PARAMAHANSA YOGANANDA AS I KNEW HIM

About the Author

Roy Eugene Davis, a direct disciple of Paramahansa Yogananda, is an internationally acclaimed teacher of meditation and spiritual growth processes, an author whose books have been published in ten languages, and the founder of Center for Spiritual Awareness with world headquarters in northeast Georgia.

PARAMAHANSA YOGANANDA
As I Knew Him

Experiences, Observations, and Reflections
of a Disciple

Roy Eugene Davis

CSA Press / Lakemont, Georgia

ISBN 0-87707-293-0

CSA Press
P.O. Box 7
Lakemont, Georgia 30552-0001

Telephone 706-782-4723
Fax 706-782-4560
e-mail: csainc@csa-davis.org
web site: www.csa-davis.org

CSA Press is the publishing department
of Center for Spiritual Awareness.

PRINTED IN THE UNITED STATES OF AMERICA

There is a fundamental purpose for our lives.
We must look beyond our immediate goals to what
we ultimately want to accomplish, and consider
life's highest potential for development.

— *Paramahansa Yogananda*

Other Books by the Author Published by CSA Press

The Science of Self-Realization
(Patanjali's Yoga-Sutras)

Seven Lessons in Conscious Living
(Kriya Yoga Philosophy and Practices)

The Eternal Way
(The Inner Meaning of the Bhagavad Gita)

A Master Guide to Meditation

Satisfying Our Innate Desire to Know God

An Easy Guide to Ayurveda

Several of Mr. Davis' books are published in India by:
Motilal Banarsidass
40-41 U.A., Bungalow Road
Jawahar Nagar
Delhi 110 007
e-mail: mlbd@vsnl.com
web site: www.mlbd.com

Contents

Preface

I am often asked what it was like to be with Paramahansa Yogananda.

He was calm, attentive, kind, patient, often humorous, and sometimes jovial. His sincere interest in the spiritual well-being of others was obvious. When concentrating on his many projects for the benefit of others he was practical and innovative, yet somewhat detached as though playing a role. He was very wise.

When I was with him, and at all other times when I attuned my mind and consciousness with his, which he frequently advised me to do, my mind was calm; I felt secure and peaceful; my awareness was tranquil and clear; I was more Self- and God-conscious.

Now, fifty-six years after meeting my guru, memories of that occasion and of all my other times with him are as vivid as though they occurred a few moments ago. In the following pages I have shared what he said to me and to others, described a few of my experiences, and provided information that I hope will be of value to readers who are devoted to their spiritual path.

Some of my perceptions and observations of my guru, what he was like, who he was, and what he taught, are different from those that have been described by a few of his other disciples because our experiences were not the same. In this book, I portray Paramahansa Yogananda *as I knew him.*

My guru's outlook was universal. Regarding the varied philosophical opinions of others, he often remarked, "The world is a big place; there is room in it for everyone."

Our world is much different than it was in the middle of the last century. Scientific discoveries have enabled us to better understand our relationship with the universe, and many technological inventions now directly influence our lives. More than four billion people have been added to the global population, an increasing number of whom are sincerely interested in conserving our planet's resources, being involved in cooperative endeavors that can benefit everyone, and nurturing authentic spiritual growth.

ROY EUGENE DAVIS

March 2005
Lakemont, Georgia

Notes

Refer to the Glossary for word-meanings and explanations of philosophical concepts. Read the Chapter Notes for information about some individuals who are mentioned in the text and elaboration on some of the themes.

In the text, I refer to Paramahansa Yogananda as Master, as did most of his disciples. A master (Latin *magister*) is a person who is acknowledged as being proficient in a branch of learning or has unique skills or abilities.

Pronunciation guide:
Par-um-hawn-sa Yog-ananda

In the Chapter Notes: *Paramahansaji.* The suffix *ji* ("gee") is used to denote respect.

Introduction

The Philosophical Principles, Traditions, and Essential Practices of Yoga

The philosophical foundation upon which the practice of yoga is based comprises four interrelated concepts. An intellectual grasp of these concepts can be helpful to the person who is intent on being Self- and God-realized.

1. Unchanging, impersonal laws of cause and effect determine the events that occur in the realm of Nature and that result from our modes of thinking, feeling, and behavior. When we know and cooperate with them, the Power that pervades the cosmos is inclined to be supportive of our aspirations and right actions.

2. A supreme Consciousness, commonly referred to as God, projects a vibrating Power (Om) that produces space, time, and fine cosmic forces which are further projected as the subtle and gross aspects of a universe. The realm of Nature is produced and maintained by orderly interactions of cosmic forces. Transformative evolutionary processes are driven by the urge of Consciousness to be expressive.

3. The pure aspect of supreme Consciousness devoid of attributes, that is not fully comprehended by the intellect, can be intuitively discerned and directly experienced and known. The expressive aspect has attributes which make world manifestation possible. The true Self (core-essence) of people and creatures was individualized by interactions between the pure essence of supreme Consciousness and the Om vibration. Souls, units of pure consciousness with blurred, fragmented awareness, have

never been, nor can ever be, separated from their Source. It is only their acquired habit of identifying their attention and awareness with modified mental states and objective phenomena that causes and sustains the illusion (faulty perception) of independent existence. When this error in perception is corrected, one's consciousness is immediately restored to its pure state.

4. The culmination of right, diligent spiritual practice is liberation of consciousness: absence of erroneous ideas, mistaken perceptions, and all influences that confined and modified it. While partial understanding of higher realities or occasional episodes of God-communion may enable one to experience a more comfortable human existence, they do not result in Self- and God-realization and liberation of consciousness. For rapid awakening through the stages of spiritual growth to be experienced, one's spiritual practice must be intensive or concentrated. Progress will be slow, faster, or rapid in accord with the intensiveness of practice and the capacity to be conscious. Learning, and awakening to Self- and God-realization, are rapid when one's attention and endeavors are focused on matters which are essential and all that is not relevant to the accomplishment of one's aims is minimized or ignored.

I often heard Paramahansa Yogananda say that spiritual evolution can be quickened by concentrated endeavor that condenses one's experiences. To *condense* something is to make it concise or specific. Concentrated endeavor enables more that is of value to be accomplished in a much shorter duration of time.

The Practices and Traditions of Yoga

Yoga is the complete bringing together (unification) of attention and awareness with one's essence of being and supreme Consciousness (God). Because, as units of pure consciousness, we have never been separated from God, there is no need to try to make a connection with God. If this is not known, our understanding of our relationship with God can be improved. This can be done by growing to emotional maturity, replacing erroneous ideas about God with accurate knowledge of God, and applying effective spiritual practices that purify the mind, clarify awareness, and restore our consciousness to wholeness.

Yoga practices evolved in Asia more than five thousand years ago as a means to quicken psychological transformation and unveil and actualize innate spiritual capacities and powers. A practitioner of these procedures needs to know the difference between *ordinary awareness* and *consciousness. Ordinary awareness* always has an object of perception that it reflects to one's *consciousness*, the medium through which awareness operates. A person who does not yet know this difference is inclined to identify with ordinary states of awareness and the ever-changing conditions of conventional existence. The purpose of yoga practice is to know the difference between *ordinary awareness* and *consciousness* and to detach consciousness from all objective and subjective conditions which modify it.

The key to Self-knowing is to quiet the changes that usually occur in the mind and awareness. This can be done by dispassionate observation of objective and subjective events and by regularly practicing meditation to the stage of superconsciousness: a clear state of consciousness that is superior to ordinary waking states, dreams, and sleep. These methods are systematically described in the yoga-sutras written by Patanjali approximately two thousand years ago. *Sutras* are "threads" of concisely presented concepts which are to be insightfully contemplated until they are fully understood. The text begins with a statement in which the author declares that what is being presented is in accord with an ancient tradition.

In the first chapter of Patanjali's treatise, superconscious (samadhi) states are described along with how they can be realized. The obstacles to be overcome by a practitioner of yoga are the subliminal influences that cause wavelike movements in the mind and awareness that result in mental confusion, interfere with concentration, and blur and fragment one's awareness. In Patanjali's text, the words *samadhi* (*sam*, to bring together) and *yoga* (union) have the same meaning. This is evident in the second sutra of Chapter Two:

yogah-chitta-vritti-nirodha
oneness–awareness-changes-restrain and stop

Yoga (samadhi) results when movements
and changes in awareness cease.

There are two distinct stages of samadhi: oneness that is supported by an object of perception; oneness that does not have the support of an object of perception.

During the first stage, attention and awareness are so fully identified with a subjective perception of light, bliss, joy, the Om vibration or other subtle sounds, or a vivid sense of communion with a larger Reality, that all sense of egocentric self is absent. This kind of samadhi leaves impressions in the mind which enable one to remember it.

During the second stage, attention and awareness are detached from objects of perception. Experience and knowledge of one's true nature as a spiritual being can then be actualized.

Beyond these two stages is the final stage during which one is constantly Self-knowing when meditating and when observing, thinking, attending to duties, and appropriately relating to events and circumstances without reverting to ordinary states of awareness.

Oneness-consciousness constantly prevails at the core of our being where we are always serenely Self-knowing and aware of our relationship with the wholeness of life. Oneness-consciousness is our original state of consciousness to be reclaimed or "remembered" rather than attained.

Even when samadhi can be easily experienced during meditation, or prevails after meditation, one should not presume that the ultimate aim of spiritual practice has been accomplished. One may still have false beliefs to discard or dormant subconscious inclinations that have yet to be neutralized.

When awareness is ordinary before Self-realization is actualized, one should affirm "I am an immortal, spiritual being" rather than "I am a human being trying to become an immortal, spiritual being."

During interludes of meditative contemplation, patient inquiry can elicit liberating insight. At such times, the most useful question to ask is "What am I?" Only a little practice of this kind of contemplation will enable one to know that the mind that one uses is not what one is, nor is one the body that was born and will die. When all that one cannot be is discarded, what remains is what one is: a perceiver and knower of what is observed.

Real yoga practice is repeated practice of samadhi until Self-knowing is constant. All that is done prior to samadhi practice is preparatory.

Meditation practice can include pranayama that calms the mind and allows the body's life forces (pranas) to flow freely; contemplation of and absorption of attention and awareness in Om; meditation on transcendental realities; devotion to God; or contemplation on any object or ideal that is pleasing to the practitioner. The purpose of right practice is to detach attention and awareness from what one is not until one's essence of being is realized. The importance of *right practice* is emphasized because endeavor that is not effective is not useful.

In the second chapter of Patanjali's treatise, intensive Kriya Yoga practice is emphasized. *Kriyas* are "actions" which can unite attention and awareness with one's pure-conscious essence. The five preliminary practices include ethical, moral behaviors; harmlessness; truthfulness; honesty; conservation and transmutation of vital forces; and avoidance of tenacious attachments of all kinds. The five fundamental disciplines are: personal cleanliness; contentment in all circumstances; mental, emotional, and behavioral discipline; Self-inquiry; and surrender of the illusional sense of self to allow one's true Self to be discerned. These disciplines provide a firm foundation for spiritual practice.

Meditation is described as sitting in a comfortable posture; pranayama; inward turning of attention; concentration on a chosen object or ideal to be realized; unwavering concentration; and having attention and awareness absorbed in the object or aim of meditation.

Because attentive Kriya Yoga practice weakens and removes the obstacles which may interfere with the emergence of innate knowledge, it is extolled as the fast, direct way to awaken to Self- and God-realization that is suitable for anyone who sincerely aspires to be spiritually enlightened. The obstacles to be removed are those which modify and fragment the mind and awareness: erroneous beliefs; illusions; fantasy; moods; and subliminal tendencies that influence awareness, thinking, behavior, and states of consciousness, or have the potential to be influential. Even when the mind can be calmed and subliminal tendencies can be pacified by an act of will or when meditating to the stage of samadhi, as long as dormant subliminal tendencies have the potential to be activated and to be troublesome, more mental purification is needed. Frequent samadhi practice weakens and removes troublesome subliminal influences.

A Kriya Yoga practitioner may adhere to the tenets of a religious faith or may choose not to do so. When the mind is fully illumined and perceptions of higher realities are flawless, former beliefs and modes of worship which may have been supportive will be transcended.

In the third chapter of Patanjali's treatise, some of the exceptional powers (*siddhis*) of perception and functional abilities one may become aware of having are described. While these can be wisely used to improve one's personal circumstances and to live effectively, they are primarily to be used to master meditative, superconscious states.

In the fourth chapter, liberation of consciousness and the means by which it can be permanently realized are described. When all that one can do to purify the mind and to clarify awareness has been done, the final awakening occurs spontaneously.

Many readers of Paramahansa Yogananda's writings presume that his emphasis on Kriya Yoga practice was that of a pranayama technique used to circulate life force through the spine and brain. While he frequently referred to this practice as Kriya Yoga, he taught all of the practices that are described in the yoga-sutras.

Most of the people who ask me to teach them Kriya Yoga do not know that disciplined thinking and behaviors, profound Self-inquiry, and awakening from the mistaken sense of Self are necessary if one is to effectively practice Kriya Yoga. Use of meditation techniques can be helpful because they calm the mind and allow contemplation to flow smoothly.

The holistic lifestyle guidelines and meditation methods described in the yoga-sutras are those of the classical Raja Yoga system. The other classical systems are Hatha, Bhakti, Karma, and Jnana Yoga.

Adherents of Hatha Yoga practice a variety of postures (*asanas*), pranayamas, and procedures that can contribute to physical well-being and provide a degree of control of the mind and body as preparation for meditation practice. Of the estimated twenty million people (as of 2002) in the United States who practice some form of yoga, Hatha Yoga has the largest number of adherents. Two basic texts on Hatha Yoga are *Shiva Samhita* and *Hatha Yoga Pradipika*.

Bhakti (devotional love) Yoga adherents endeavor to express compassion and kindness toward everyone while being devoted to God-realization. Adherents of this path should avoid allowing sentimental feelings or emotions to interfere with rational thinking or to influence their behaviors.

Karma Yoga practice requires skillful performance of duties (and all other actions) without attachment to them or their results. One is then no longer unduly influenced by the effects of past thoughts or actions or by transitory events that occur. The words *karma* and *kriya* are derived from the Sanskrit verb root "to do"—to cause an event to occur. *Karma* is usually considered as ordinary causative influences: one's thoughts, desires, inclinations, intentions, actions, and subconscious tendencies of which one may or may not be aware. *Kriyas* are intentional actions implemented to quicken psychological transformation; calm and purify the mind; improve one's intellectual and intuitive powers; resist, weaken, and eliminate troublesome subconscious influences; refine the brain and nervous system; clarify awareness; and allow the practitioner's spiritual capacities to be unveiled and actualized.

Jnana (*gyana*, knowledge) Yoga practice is appropriate for truth seekers whose intellectual and intuitive powers are, or can be, highly developed. Philosophical concepts are insightfully examined, valid knowledge is acquired, what is not true is discarded, intuitive insights occur, and the facts of life are directly perceived as innate knowledge of one's true Self in relationship with the Infinite emerges.

A *tradition* is the transmittal of cultural elements and useful knowledge from one generation to another, usually by oral communication. In the Kriya Yoga tradition which I represent as a disciple of Paramahansa Yogananda, all of the useful practices of the classical systems are taught in accord with the learner's psychological temperament and capacity to practice. Proficiency in meditation practice is emphasized, as is sustained aspiration to be Self- and God-realized demonstrated by total commitment to practice.

Kriya Yoga practices are ideal for truth seekers in our current era because the intellectual and intuitive powers of human beings are increasing and more people are able to understand and appreciate the philosophical concepts upon which they are based. Practitioners are advised to frequently read Patanjali's yoga-sutras and a commentary on the Bhagavad Gita that provides an explanation of its esoteric (inner) meaning.

We are in this world for only a brief duration of time. We are here to learn how to live effectively—and do it—and to awaken to Self- and God-realization. The four primary aims of life to successfully accomplish are:

1. To live in harmony with the physical and metaphysical laws of cause and effect while using our knowledge and skills to enhance our lives and the lives of others.
2. To have necessary desires easily fulfilled.
3. To always have the material resources we need for our well-being and to accomplish purposes that are of value.
4. To awaken to liberation of consciousness.

The Practical Usefulness of Discipleship

All yoga traditions emphasize the usefulness of having a *guru* (teacher). A guru should be both knowledgeable and competent as a result of his or her own prior practice, for only a teacher who has experienced the results of right living and meditation practice is qualified to guide others.

A *disciple* is a "learner" or "student." The easiest way to acquire accurate information is to obtain it from others who are already knowledgeable. Newly acquired knowledge should be tested by personal experience to verify its usefulness. Knowledge that is not used is of little value. Many people who have read metaphysical books and attended churches, seminars, and meditation retreats for decades, have not yet experienced satisfying spiritual growth or obvious improvements of circumstances. They may lack knowledge of how to help themselves or they may not have used the knowledge that they acquired.

A common mistake that some disciples make is to hope that their newly acquired metaphysical knowledge or their interludes of passive, inattentive meditation will enable them to experience improvements in their life without having to outgrow ordinary states of awareness. They may want the positive results of right endeavor and spiritual growth without having to change their habitual ways of thinking and behaving.

A person with a strong sense of individualism (of will and personality) can succeed as a disciple if their will to learn and to grow to emotional and spiritual maturity is wisely directed and they are willing to allow their inclination to be overly assertive to be moderated by humility. Absence of egotism enables one to acknowledge that their mistaken sense of self is an illusion to be renounced or transcended. If the sense of individualism is so strong that they insist on dramatizing an inflated sense of self-importance, they may resist learning and have difficulty accepting new ideas or wise counsel that require them to modify or renounce assertive, ego-driven behaviors.

Emotionally immature individuals who are interested in discipleship may lack a sense of self-worth, have doubts about their ability to control thoughts and behaviors, or be inclined to want to have a dependent relationship with a teacher, or with God.

Some characteristics and capacities that can enable a person to benefit from discipleship are:

• Sincerity. With pure motives and no inclination to merely pretend to be interested in learning.

• Willingness to learn. Discipleship requires an open-minded mental attitude, ability to discern truth from untruth, quick acceptance of useful information, and constructive behaviors.
• Intelligence to understand philosophical concepts and whatever else one may need to know.
• Rational thinking along with the ability to make right choices and wisely use imagination and will power.
• Absence of mental perversity (a neurotic inclination to distort or use what is learned for egocentric purposes).
• Respect for the teachings and the teachers of a tradition of spiritual practice that is of value.
• Total commitment to ethical living, metaphysical study, and intensive spiritual practice. Discipleship will not be useful for a person who does not adhere to wholesome lifestyle regimens, is inclined to be preoccupied with useless philosophical speculation or fantasy, or is only mildly interested in being spiritually enlightened.

A cloistered or monastic environment is not necessary for discipleship. Some people can thrive in such an environment; others become neurotically preoccupied with self-centered interests. Most spiritual aspirants can make satisfactory progress by living a wholesome, balanced life with duties to perform and opportunities to appropriately relate to others, fulfill useful desires, and grow to emotional maturity.

What is most important for a disciple is to live a well-ordered life, meditate superconsciously, and be aware of abiding in the wholeness of God. It can also be helpful to schedule occasional private retreats in a quiet place that is conducive to physical and mental renewal, where ordinary duties and concerns can be temporarily ignored, and meditation can be more intensively practiced.

Constant personal association with one's guru is not always

necessary. After philosophical concepts and lifestyle and spiritual practice routines have been learned, the disciple's responsibility is to apply what has been learned. Communication between the teacher and student should occur when the student needs further instruction or guidance. The teacher's role is to encourage the student to grow to emotional and spiritual maturity and awaken to Self- and God-realization. A person who is satisfied with a modest degree of improvement of personal circumstances or with enjoyable meditative perceptions rather than authentic, transformative spiritual growth is not yet ready for discipleship.

For a teacher-student (guru-disciple) relationship to be of real value, communication between them must actually occur. It should not be avoided by the student when the teacher is accessible, nor should it be only imagined to exist or presumed to be telepathic.

I receive telephone calls and e-mail from individuals who say they have visions of Paramahansa Yogananda, or other spiritual teachers who are no longer in the body, and are being guided by them. They then tell me that they are confused or have personal problems over which they have little or no control. If they had direct, meaningful contact with a spiritually enlightened teacher they would not be confused or constantly have troublesome circumstances. Because they are inclined to fantasize, they do not always think rationally and are not willing to assume responsibility for their thoughts, behaviors, and circumstances.

The desire to be spiritually awake can more easily be fulfilled by daily, right practice of meditation that calms the mind, and unwavering aspiration to be Self-realized nurtured by faith that it will be accomplished.

My guru often said, "Devotion is more important than practice of meditation techniques; together, they are an unbeatable combination."

A person whose psychological temperament is mainly devotional may think that intellectual analysis of higher realities is not necessary or may neglect superconscious meditation practice. One who is inclined to intellectually examine philosophical concepts and to meditate, may need to be reminded of the usefulness of nurturing devotion.

Because spiritual awakening occurs more easily when the body is healthy, the mind is well-ordered, emotions are stable, environmental conditions are supportive, personal relationships are ideal, behaviors are well-disciplined, and actions are constructively purposeful, everything that one does should be viewed as spiritual practice. If ordinary states of consciousness are allowed to prevail or thoughts and behaviors are allowed to be influenced by moods, whims, or subconscious inclinations, meditation is not likely to be transformative.

The Purpose, Significance, and Value of Initiation

When a disciple is willing to be fully committed to right living and spiritual practice, initiation can be offered, which may be a simple affair or may include a formal ceremony. Initiation is a rite of passage into a body of knowledge and the company of adherents of that knowledge. The occasion of initiation should be known as a "new beginning" that empowers the disciple to more quickly fulfill his or her spiritual destiny.

Awakening to Self- and God-realization to the stage of liberation of consciousness should be considered as being possible in one's current incarnation rather than as a goal to be accomplished in the distant future, as one leaves the body, in an imagined astral realm, or during another physical incarnation.

At the time of initiation, one is instructed to be committed to ethical living and spiritual practice, and meditation methods may be taught. In the Kriya Yoga tradition represented by Mahavatar Babaji, Lahiri Mahasaya, Sri Yukteswar, Paramahansa Yogananda, and their successors, initiates are taught a unique pranayama and supplemental meditation methods which are to be regularly practiced. When conditions are ideal, the guru's consciousness is blended with the disciple's consciousness and a spiritual force is transmitted that can awaken the disciple's dormant soul forces. A psychic (soul) connection is then permanently established between the guru and the disciple that enables the disciple who nurtures it to be receptive to streams of supportive, redemptive grace that flow through the guru and the lineage of gurus.

The spiritual bond between the guru and the disciple is maintained and strengthened when the disciple adheres to spiritual practices as taught by the guru. The bond may be weakened if the disciple allows distractions to interfere with it. Harmonious mental and spiritual attunement with one's guru enables the relationship to be of the greatest spiritual value to the disciple.

I was initiated by Paramahansa Yogananda during the summer of 1950. In 1951, in late autumn, he ordained me to teach and to initiate others.

PARAMAHANSA YOGANANDA
As I Knew Him

CHAPTER ONE

Beginnings

When I was a child, I had frequent glimpses of higher realities and was often vividly aware of an all-pervading, benevolent Presence that included me and all things in its wholeness. Perceptions of this kind are not uncommon among young people who, having newly arrived in the physical world, have not yet been unduly influenced by the ideas or behaviors of others.

I was born shortly after midnight on March 9, 1931, in Leavittsburg, Ohio, south of Cleveland, the fourth of five children and the second son. When I was six years of age, my family moved to a forty-five acre farm in Braceville Township, Trumbull County, where I grew up and attended school. For two years after we moved to the farm we did not have the convenience of electric power. Kerosene lamps were used to light our house at night. A basement coal and wood burning furnace provided heat during winter months. Food was cooked on a large cast-iron kitchen stove. Water was drawn from an open well and carried to the house in buckets.

My father, DeWitt Talmage Davis, was named after a then prominent midwest clergyman because his mother had wanted him to be a minister. His paternal grandfather had immigrated from Wales; his maternal grandfather was a Native American, of which tribe I am not certain. My mother, Eva Lee Davis, was born in Kentucky and married my father in southern Ohio in the early 1920s.

My childhood was normal. Farm chores were assigned at an early age. I played with my friends, swam in nearby creeks during the summer months, walked in the woods, enjoyed riding my horse during my teenage years, and helped with the planting and harvesting of field crops.

With my family, I regularly attended Sunday services at a local United Brethren Church[1] where "sinners" in the congregation were regularly advised to "repent and be saved." Though inspired by some of the Bible stories, I was not impressed by fundamentalist doctrines, nor did I believe them to be true. I did, however, during my teenage years, experience a compelling sense of being called to the ministry in a more universal way. In my mind's eye, I saw myself traveling throughout the world to tell others about God and their innate capacity to know God.

During my senior high school year, I experienced a few episodes of minor discomfort due to occasional strep throat infections. In February, 1949, my illness was diagnosed by our family doctor as rheumatic fever and I was told that I must stay in bed until my health was restored. Thus began five months of seclusion which were to provide me with many opportunities to nourish my mind, expand my consciousness, discover the Kriya Yoga path, and know with certainty the major purpose for my life.

I had already read many books that I borrowed from the County Library. Books on psychology and religious movements appealed to me, as did some poems by Alfred Lord Tennyson and the writings of Ralph Waldo Emerson, Henry David Thoreau, and Walt Whitman. I learned about yoga practices while reading Francis Yeats-Brown's *Lives of a Bengal Lancer*, Paul Brunton's *Search in Secret India*, and Theos Bernard's *Hatha Yoga*. I began to practice Hatha Yoga, which I could easily do, and tried to meditate. Alone, in my upstairs bedroom, I sometimes sat on the floor in the lotus posture and imagined that I was a spiritually accomplished Himalayan yogi.

While I was confined to bed, I read articles in health-oriented magazines that motivated me to choose a vegetarian diet. In one magazine, I saw an advertisement for *Autobiography of a Yogi*[2] by Paramahansa Yogananda, published by Self-Realization Fellowship, and ordered a copy by mail. As soon as I received it, I read it, then read it frequently. As I avidly perused the text and looked at the pictures of saints and yogis, I knew that Paramahansa Yogananda was my guru.

Weekly printed lessons in which meditation methods were explained were available from Self-Realization Fellowship and I requested them. Soon, I learned how to use a meditation mantra and to listen to the Om vibration.

I prayed for healing and for guidance in regard to my future circumstances. During one intensive prayer session, a surge of energy suddenly moved upward through my spine and into my brain. My spine stiffened and arched as my body became rigid for several minutes. As the force of energy subsided, I became very calm and sensed that a meaningful event had occurred. During the remaining weeks of confinement I patiently waited for my physical healing to be completed and looked forward with anticipation to what was yet to unfold. Mentally, I was already in Los Angeles with Paramahansa Yogananda.

In early July of 1949, I was allowed to leave my bed. When I looked at my reflection in a mirror, I was astonished to see how thin my body was after five months of physical inactivity. That night, my mother died of a heart attack.

The next morning, my father told me that he had seen a light emerge from my mother's face as she passed from her body. And knowing that I had been reading religious literature, he asked me to tell my six year old sister about the death of our mother. Because I knew that a physical body is a soul's temporary abode, I prayed for my mother's spiritual well-being, but was not disturbed by thoughts or feelings of loss or grief.

During the months that followed, I prepared meals for my father and younger sister, adhered to a vegetarian diet, and daily practiced Hatha Yoga and meditated.

In November, again physically strong, I felt that it was time to go to California. Thinking that I should first earn enough money for travel expenses, I impulsively decided to go to Florida to avoid another Ohio winter and to obtain temporary employment. My father, somewhat emotionally unsettled by my unexpected decision and reluctant to have me so suddenly depart, gave me a few dollars and took me to the Greyhound bus station in the nearby city of Warren.

The bus ride to Florida was a novel experience. Until then, I had not been more than two hundred miles from where I was born. In downtown Miami, I rented a room in a modest hotel for two dollars a day and soon obtained a job in a small, suburban restaurant, working in the kitchen, for which I was paid one dollar an hour and provided a noon meal. Two weeks later, lured by the prospect of more generous financial rewards, I joined a group of young men who were hired to sell magazine subscriptions.

While I was with the sales crew in West Palm Beach, going from one house to another, knocking on doors in what proved to be a vain attempt to sell magazine subscriptions, a timely event occurred. When I knocked on the door of a small house, a middle-age woman of pleasant demeanor opened the door and invited me into her kitchen for a cup of tea. When she asked about my future plans, I informed her of my intention to go to California to study with Paramahansa Yogananda. She smiled, and took me to a small room with many shelves filled with hundreds of books on philosophy and religion. She then informed me that here, William Walker Atkinson, the author of several books on yoga practices (using the name Yogi Ramacharakra) and New Thought[3] themes that were published in the early 1900s, had written some of his books. As I thanked my hostess and prepared to depart, she remarked, "If you want to be with your teacher, why don't you go now?" Her words reinforced my private thoughts.

That evening, when I informed the sales manager of my decision to go to California, he quickly agreed with my plan. I had only sold two magazine subscriptions during the previous two weeks. The next day, in Tampa, he drove me to the northern edge of the city, loaned me five dollars, and wished me well. I repaid him a few weeks later.

At a nearby grocery store, I purchased a modest quantity of peanuts, raisins, and dry, rolled oats for snacks along the way. I then stood patiently by the highway for several hours, waiting for a passing motorist to offer me a ride[4] to Tallahassee, from where I would go westward. A ride was not offered. That night I slept in an orange grove, partially warmed by a small wood fire.

Early in the morning, with a positive mental attitude, I stood by the highway. Within a few minutes, I was offered a ride to Tallahassee. Six days later, I was in Los Angeles.

In the religion-philosophy department of the Los Angeles Public Library, I read back issues of *Self-Realization* magazine and verified the SRF headquarters street address. At dusk, in need of food and rest, I walked to the nearby Fifth Street Mission, where I was provided with a hot shower, a warm meal, and a clean bed for the night.

For most of the following day, I was again in the Public Library. Late in the afternoon, I walked a few blocks to where streetcars were accessible and asked a store clerk for directions to the Highland Park district of the city. He provided the information that I needed and voluntarily gave me ten cents for streetcar fare.

Twenty minutes later, as I started to walk up a steep, winding street that led to the top of Mount Washington, a car stopped beside me. The driver, a young man, asked, "Where are you going?" When I told him, he said, "Get in. I will be going right by there. I'll drop you off at the front gate."

CHAPTER ONE NOTES

1. The United Brethren Church was a small, fundamentalist denomination that later merged with the Methodist Church.

2. *Autobiography of a Yogi* by Paramahansa Yogananda was first published in 1946. Now published in a variety of paperback and clothbound editions by Self-Realization Fellowship, it has been translated into more than twenty major world languages.

3. *New Thought* is the name of a modern religious movement with a metaphysical teaching emphasis that began to emerge in the United States in the late 1880s. Its adherents extol the ideal of spiritual well-being and the usefulness of positive thinking and constructive living. Hundreds of churches and teaching centers (Unity, Science of Mind, Religious Science, Divine Science, independent groups) in the United States and other countries serve an increasing number of people. The offices and archives of the International New Thought Alliance are in Mesa, Arizona. A magazine is published quarterly and a week long Congress at which ministers and lay members gather is held annually.

4. I do not recommend hitchhiking today.

CHAPTER TWO

Early Experiences With My Guru

I arrived at the international headquarters[1] of Self-Realization Fellowship on Friday evening, December 23, 1949, a few minutes after 6 p.m.

When I knocked on the door of a cottage just inside the driveway entrance, a man who appeared to be about sixty years of age greeted me and took me to the men's dining room in the basement level of the main building. There, I was introduced to several young resident disciples and invited to join them at their evening meal.

After supper, a young man, who I later learned was responsible for coordinating the daily work and meditation schedules of the male disciples, led me up a stairway and to a secluded area in the main entrance room where we could privately talk. He inquired about my background and asked how I had heard about the organization and Paramahansa Yogananda. Within a few minutes, when the muted sounds of a descending elevator emanated from a nearby hallway, he stood up, turned toward the hallway, and exclaimed, "Master is coming!" I also stood up and turned toward the hallway with alert anticipation.

Paramahansa Yogananda came into the room, followed by two young women disciples, Faye Wright[2] and her sister Virginia.[3] He was wearing a dark blue overcoat, a white neck scarf, and a light blue felt hat. Standing in front of me, he looked into my eyes, smiled kindly as he shook my hand with a gentle grasp, and quietly asked, "How old are you?"

"Eighteen, Sir," I responded.

"Do your parents know you are here?" he inquired.

"It's all right, Sir," I assured him.

Touching my forehead with his hand in a gesture of blessing, he murmured, "That's good. I'll talk with you again."

Then, with Faye and Virginia, he went to a dark blue Cadillac sedan that I had earlier seen in the driveway near the steps of the porch. The young man who was with me then took me outside and along a garden path to a small, one-story house that was used as a men's dormitory.

While I unpacked my suitcase, I was informed that the following morning everyone would gather in the headquarters building to attend an all-day meditation.

After a night of refreshing sleep, and breakfast, I joined the more than one hundred resident disciples and visiting SRF students who had gathered for the occasion.

Before long, as Master, accompanied by James Lynn,[4] a spiritually advanced disciple, came into the room, I noticed that he was in a superconscious state, with an aura of remoteness about him. When they had gone into the chapel, ushers invited everyone to enter and be seated.

Master spoke warm words of welcome, expressed his happiness to be with us, remarked on the significance of the Holy Season, mentioned the names of a few disciples and acknowledged their years of devotion and service, and talked about God and the lineage[5] of gurus. He referred to God as a supreme Being beyond creation and as the cosmic energy expressing in and as Nature. His settled composure established an intimate mood.

Dr. Minot Lewis,[6] at the organ, began to play one of the devotional chants that Master had, years before, adapted from those of his native land. "Chanting[7] will enable you to win half of the battle in meditation," Master said. "When you chant with fervent devotion to God, all stray thoughts will flee from your mind. Then, you will know God's presence!"

Group chanting continued for several minutes. As the final refrains faded, we were encouraged to "dive deep" in meditation. After an extended duration of silence, Master talked quietly about God and the usefulness of devotion, and led another chanting session which was followed by more silent meditation. At noon, a short rest break was announced.

During the afternoon session, as Master was talking about various aspects of God, Mr. Lynn slumped in his chair, his face suffused in a beatific glow. A few moments later, when he was again composed and sitting upright, Master chuckled softly, and said, "When I talk like this, he always goes into ecstasy."

After the six-hour meditation session, Master spoke for a few minutes and pronounced a benediction, then stood at the chapel entrance to bless each person as they departed.

On Sunday morning I attended the service at the Self-Realization Church of All Religions[8] (as it was then named) on Sunset Boulevard in Hollywood. Master lead the congregation in a responsive prayer, read a few verses from the Bhagavad Gita and The New Testament, and added a brief commentary. An interlude of devotional chanting and silent meditation preceded his sermon-lesson, which lasted about an hour. During his forthright, extemporaneous talk, he shared interesting anecdotes, mentioned some saints he had known, described some of his personal experiences, and exhorted everyone to be dedicated to the spiritual path until they were Self- and God-realized. He then asked everyone to stand up, raise their hands, and chant Om with him three times "for the healing of the body, mind, and soul."

While many people gathered around Master to talk with him and receive his blessing, Myrna Brown,[9] one of his secretaries, approached me. "Master will see you after he has seen the others who have appointments with him," she said. "I'll let you know when he's ready."

Late that afternoon, I was taken to a small room next to the stage and altar area in the temple. Master, sitting on a small couch, motioned for me to sit beside him. In a barely audible tone, he asked, "What can I do for you?"

"I want to be your disciple, Sir," I responded.

He seemed pleased. "This is not a path of escapism, you know," he quietly informed me.

"I know that, Sir," I told him.

He asked about my health. When I assured him that I felt well, he said, "Let's see," and felt my pulse at the wrist. A few moments later, he murmured, "Yes, you are all right."

He then said, "You can stay." He told me to read only his writings and some scriptures during the first year, to attend to duties that would be assigned to me, and to meditate regularly. As he touched my forehead, his concluding words were, "Read a little. Meditate more. Think of God all the time."

That evening, disciples and visiting guests gathered in the main room of the headquarters building for the annual Christmas dinner. While awaiting Master's arrival, some of them mingled in small groups to enjoy quiet interaction with friends.

Mr. Lynn approached the group of monks that I was with, introduced himself to me, and offered personal advice. He recommended that I meditate on a regular schedule for short periods of time until I could meditate comfortably, then meditate longer. He told me, "That is what I found to be helpful when I began to meditate after meeting Master."

Before long, Master came into the room, everyone was invited to be seated at long tables, and bowls and platters of food were brought from the kitchen.

After the dessert was served, Master spoke for a little more than an hour. He acknowledged the dedication of the disciples who were there and emphasized the importance of letting our desires be disciplined by wisdom. He then invited everyone to "come forward and receive God's blessings from my hands."

During the next few weeks I participated with the monks in the morning and evening routines of exercise and meditation and was attentive to my assigned duties: sweeping the sidewalks and driveways, cleaning some of the buildings, and occasionally typing portions of form letters that were sent to SRF members to whom weekly printed lessons were mailed. Evenings and weekends provided opportunities for private study and reflection. On some Saturday mornings, a few of the monks gathered for informal sessions of devotional chanting and meditation.

I also worked at the newly acquired Lake Shrine in Pacific Palisades that was being landscaped and prepared for a public dedication later that summer. Surrounding a small lake are shrines honoring some of the world's religions and secluded areas for private meditation. White towers, with gold lotus domes, serve as a central focus. Mr. Lynn donated the money for the purchase of several acres of land above the Lake Shrine. In 1996, a beautiful temple was constructed there.

At SRF headquarters, Master occasionally walked for exercise and to make suggestions regarding maintenance and improvements of the grounds and buildings. He also talked with disciples whom he encountered. During one of my random meetings with him, he said, "Be patient, Roy. I have plans for you."

One evening, I was walking by the driveway near the main building with a brother disciple. We met Master, who was out for a stroll. After a few minutes of general conversation, he handed his cane to me and his hat to the other disciple, and inhaled and exhaled deeply a few times while tensing and relaxing the muscles of his upper body. Recovering his cane and hat, he said, "See! No matter how busy I am, I always do my exercises."[10]

Someone had given the monks a table-tennis set that was temporarily put near their basement dining room. I came out of the dining room one evening as Master came into the hallway with Faye and Virginia Wright. Seeing the table-tennis table, he motioned for me to pick up a paddle. As we were gently hitting the ball back and forth a few times, a gleam came into his eyes and he suddenly sent it past me with a fast, forceful stroke of his paddle. Pleased with his performance, he said to Faye and Virginia, "And *who* used be the best table-tennis player around here?"

He then walked to the nearby elevator and entered it. A moment after the door closed, it opened again. Master looked out at me and quietly said, "You have a wonderful future, Roy."

During another evening, when Master came into the lower hallway and saw me and three other disciples, he invited himself into the men's dining room and asked for something to eat. A bowl of corn flakes with milk was prepared for him. As he was eating his light snack, he saw a small bottle of hot sauce on a cabinet shelf and asked for it. After pouring some of the hot sauce into his spoon, he tasted it, and smiled. He then said, "Line up, boys," and happily measured out a small portion for each of us while telling us that we could, with practice, learn to withdraw our attention from the senses and not feel any discomfort.

On January 5, Master's birthday, the disciples at SRF headquarters gathered in the evening to meditate with him in the chapel, after which a banquet was enjoyed by everyone. On such occasions he praised the dedication of the disciples who were consistent in their spiritual practices. In the course of his talk he said, "Among those who are here tonight, many will be jivanmuktas and some will be siddhas."

A *jivanmukta* is soul- (*jiva*) free (*mukta*), Self-realized, with subliminal tendencies (karmic conditions) yet to be eliminated. *Siddhas* (accomplished) yogis are fully liberated from all conditions that formerly blurred and confined their consciousness.

During the first two months that I was with Master, I became increasingly aware of a deeper relationship that was being established between us. Although he had not yet formally accepted me as his disciple, he related to me as he did to his disciples. I experienced direct transmission of knowledge from him, and was sometimes able to intuit his thoughts and anticipate his comments before he spoke them to me or to others. When I discerned his unspoken thoughts, he would glance at me with a knowing smile. When I was not physically with him, I was often mentally and spiritually attuned to his mind and consciousness and "felt" his presence.

Strong energy movements occurred in my body within a few weeks after I met Master. Unexpected surges of life force would quickly ascend the spinal pathway, then subside. When I sat to meditate, the flows became more pronounced. If I was not relaxed when the process occurred, my body would sometimes be pulled upright. A brother disciple noticed these occasional movements and asked about them. When I described the sensations, he smiled. "It's because of your frequent contact with Master and because you are in this environment," he explained. "It happened to me when I first came here, too."

When a receptive disciple has a personal relationship with a spiritually awake person, dormant forces are aroused within the disciple to the degree that one is receptive. This can occur spontaneously or the guru may intentionally transmit life force to the disciple. By experimenting, I discovered that when I was relaxed during meditation, the energy surges would flow freely without causing a physical reaction. Instead, a mild ecstasy was experienced.

A few days after my arrival at SRF headquarters, an older disciple became ill. I was asked to take his meals to his room. He had said to another disciple, "I have respect for Master, but I don't have the faith that you boys seem to have. I wish I did."

When his condition did not improve, he was taken to a hospital. Master went to see him and returned at a late hour. I was at the lower entrance of the main building with a few monks when he arrived. He told us, "I asked him, 'Do you want to live? If you do, tell me right now and I will heal[11] you.' He said, 'No, Sir.' He has lost his will to live and I couldn't help him. If he had said 'yes' I could have healed him and he would have had a few more years to make spiritual progress. It was sad to see him like that."

Late one evening, Master talked privately with me in the living room of his modest, two-room apartment on the top floor of the headquarters building. As he blessed me, and assured me that he would talk with me from time to time, he took a banana from a nearby bowl of fruit and gave it to me. In the men's dormitory a few minutes later, sitting on my bed, reflecting on my good fortune to have Master as my guru, I slowly ate the banana, including the peel because I did not want to deprive myself of any blessings that flowed from his hands.

A new building, which Master named India House, was then being built beside the Hollywood temple. A vegetarian restaurant would be at the street level; a meeting hall at the lower level would be used for social and cultural purposes. When the concrete walls were being poured, all of the monks were assigned to the project. Bernard Cole,[12] a senior SRF minister, came late in the afternoon to examine the work in progress. As he walked by me, he said, "Master wants to see you tonight. Be in the basement hallway near the elevator at seven o'clock."

At 9 p.m., after I had waited for two hours, thinking that Master had been detained because of other, more important matters, I went to the dormitory and slept.

"Where were you last night?" The unexpected inquiry was directed to me by one of the younger monks. "Master had to go out last night and got back late. He asked me 'Where's Roy?' When I offered to find you, he said he would see you later."

That afternoon, Bernard informed me, "Master wants to see you tonight at seven o'clock, in the lower hallway."

That evening, after I had patiently waited for almost two hours, Master's car was brought to the entrance of the building and luggage was put into its trunk. Word spread that he was going to his retreat house in Twentynine Palms, a three hour drive east of Los Angeles, and would be there for several months.

Thirty or more disciples lined the hallway to bid their guru a fond farewell. Before long, someone announced that Master was talking on the telephone and would not depart until the next day. His car was returned to the garage, the gathering of disciples dispersed, and I was again alone, this time firmly resolved to remain there throughout the night, if necessary. I did not have to wait long.

I heard the elevator descend, and stop. As the door slid open, Master looked out, saw me, smiled broadly, and exuberantly exclaimed, "There's my boy!"

"Come with me," he invited, as he quickly walked to Bernard's nearby room.

Master, dressed to go for a walk, was nibbling from a handful of almonds. Catching my eye, he remarked, "This is the only food I've eaten today."

In Bernard's room, Master asked me to kneel before him and held my right hand in his. In a gentle, paternal tone of voice, he said, "Years ago, when Sri Yukteswar accepted me as a disciple, he told me, 'I pledge to you my eternal, unconditional love. No matter what you do, or fail to do, I will love you forever.'" Grasping my hand more firmly, he said, "Roy, I pledge to you my eternal, unconditional love. Can you pledge that same love to me?"

"Yes, Sir," I assured him.

When I stood up, he inquired, "Will you do as I ask?"

My response was immediately affirmative.

"I want you to go to Phoenix. We have a new project there. The climate will be good for your health, too. Bernard will take you to the train station in the morning."

He told me to write to him frequently and to visit him every two months.

CHAPTER TWO NOTES

1. The international headquarters of Self-Realization Fellowship is located at 3880 San Rafael Avenue, Los Angeles, California. In India: Yogoda Satsanga Math, Dakshineswar, Kolkata, West Bengal.

2. Faye Wright (Daya Mata, 1914 –) was seventeen years of age when she first met Paramahansa Yogananda in 1931 when she attended his lectures in Salt Lake City, Utah. Shortly thereafter, she moved to southern California to live at the SRF center in Los Angeles. She and her sister Virginia worked closely with their guru for many years: processing his correspondence, scheduling his appointments, and involved in a variety of organizational projects. The president of Self-Realization Fellowship since 1955, she has been diligently instrumental in having many of Paramahansa Yogananda's organizational projects completed. Her monastic name, Daya Mata (compassionate mother), is compatible with her caring demeanor and warm personality.

3. Virginia Wright (Ananda Mata, 1915 – 2005) was also a member of the Board of Directors and Secretary-Treasurer of the organization.

Richard Wright (1911 – 2002), a brother, traveled to India with Paramahansa Yogananda in the mid-1930s. Some of his diary notes are published in *Autobiography of a Yogi* (Chapters 40-42).

4. James Lynn (1882 – 1955) was born near Archibald, Louisiana. His father worked on a cotton farm. At age fourteen James Lynn was also working. When he was seventeen, he traveled by train to Kansas City. There, he found a job, completed his high school education, went to law school, and studied accounting. He was admitted to the bar and became a certified public accountant in his twenty-first year. He married in 1913 and was employed as an accountant for the U.S. Epperson Underwriting Company. He was soon promoted to the position of general manager. A few years later, with the help of a large loan from a friendly bank officer, he bought the company. He later formed another insurance company, invested in railroad and bank stocks, bought a citrus grove in Texas, and leased thousands of acres in Louisiana and Texas where he successfully drilled for oil. In the 1940s his businesses were producing many millions of dollars.

    Mr. Lynn's residence in Kansas City was on one hundred acres of wooded land with a nine-hole golf course. Successful in business endeavors, he was still restless and not completely satisfied with his life.

In January 1932, Paramahansa Yogananda visited Kansas City to present a series of lectures and classes. During one of the lectures that Mr. Lynn attended, he noticed that he became very calm and relaxed. During the days that followed, before going to his business office he went to Paramahansaji's hotel room to talk and meditate with him. After he was initiated, the first time he practiced kriya pranayama he experienced an ecstatic state of consciousness.

While continuing to be successful in his business ventures, Mr. Lynn maintained a regular schedule of holistic lifestyle regimens and meditation practice. As often as possible, he traveled to California to be with his guru and to meditate. His generous donations through the years helped to provide a firm financial foundation for Self-Realization Fellowship. In the 1930s, he purchased the Encinitas oceanfront property that is now an SRF retreat center and had a Hermitage built on it while Paramahansaji was in India. In the early 1950s he donated money to enable SRF to buy the property on which the Lake Shrine temple was later built, gave one million dollars of Kansas City Southern Railway stock, and designated that two million dollars be given after his wife's death (which occurred circa 1965).

While he was the president of SRF (1952-55), he sold his various businesses and moved permanently to Borrego Springs, north of San Diego, where his hired workers planted and harvested a variety of organic fruits and vegetables on his newly acquired 640-acre farm.

In 1952, while I was the minister of the Phoenix, Arizona, Self-Realization Center, Faye Wright informed me in a letter that Mr. Lynn was recovering from a surgical procedure that had been done to remove a benign tumor from his brain. Mr. Lynn's doctors and nurses were impressed by his calm demeanor, clarity of awareness, and absence of any indication of pain or discomfort. After a third surgical procedure, in October 1954, his immune system became weaker. On February 20, 1955, at 4 a.m., he peacefully left his body.

5.   Information about the lineage of gurus of this Kriya Yoga tradition is in the Appendix of this book.

6.   Dr. Minot Lewis (1893 – 1960) met Paramahansa Yogananda in Boston in 1920. Until he retired from the practice of dentistry in 1945

and moved to the SRF center in Encinitas, he conducted regular meditation classes and traveled often to California to be with his guru. During his later years, he lectured and taught classes at the SRF temple in
San Diego. On April 7, 1960, he was admitted to Scripps Memorial
Hospital in La Jolla, California, for tests for a heart condition. On April
13, in the early evening, with his wife, Mildred, visiting him, he sat on
his bed to meditate. A few minutes later, he withdrew from his body.

7. Recent studies have demonstrated that repetitive chanting of a
short, simple melody can reduce stress, calm the mind, and produce
interactions between the hemispheres of the brain which enable one to
meditate more effectively.

8. The Hollywood Self-Realization Fellowship Temple is at 4860 Sunset Boulevard. The SRF Lake Shrine and Temple in Pacific Palisades
is at 17190 Sunset Boulevard, less than a quarter of a mile from the
Pacific Coast Highway.

9. Myrna Brown (Mrinalini Mata, circa 1931 –) met Paramahansaji
in the middle 1940s, in the San Diego area, during her early teenage
years. She has been responsible for editing SRF books and publications and has been vice-president of the Board of Directors since 1966.

10. The "energization exercises" innovated by Paramahansa Yogananda
consist of mild tensing of one's muscles and regulated breathing, while
willing life force to flow from the medulla oblongata at the base of the
brain to the muscles that are being used. The exercises improve muscle
strength, vitalize the body, and reduce stress.

11. During his public lectures in the 1920s, Paramahansaji sometimes
demonstrated his healing methods which included prayer, affirmation,
visualization, concentrated will power, and conscious direction of life
forces. He emphasized exercise, a vegetarian diet, and meditation practice. Many people were also healed by his silent work on their behalf.

12. Bernard Cole (1922 – circa 1979) met Paramahansa Yogananda in
1939 and was a Self-Realization Fellowship minister in the late 1940s
and early 1950s. He left the organization in 1955 to teach indepen-
dently for a while and worked for several years in the fields of electron-
ics and engineering.

CHAPTER THREE

Observations and Reflections
of a Disciple

In Phoenix, I was met by Herbert Freed,[1] the minister of the
SRF Center[2] which had been dedicated by Master in the late
1940s. Located at 1800 West Monroe Street, two blocks from the
State Capitol, the one-story house had four modest rooms, and a
chapel in which Sunday evening and midweek services were conducted.

Bernard's mother was visiting Phoenix for a few days and
had prepared a light meal. At the kitchen table, Herbert told me
about the "new project"—a goat dairy.

The Rosebud Goat Dairy, approximately three miles from
Scottsdale, Arizona, then a one-stoplight village, had been funded
by Mr. Lynn. A small house, one barn, and a herd of twenty goats
were on the five-acre site. A few weeks after my arrival, three
adobe brick barns were built and, to increase milk production,
eighty goats were purchased from a California dairy.

I arranged a small altar in a corner of my private room. Before dawn and late at night, I sat there and meditated. I used the
techniques that I had learned and applied the helpful advice that
Master had given to me and which I had heard him give to others. My meditations became more consistently satisfying, and I
devoted two or three hours a day to practice.

Many interesting meditative perceptions occurred. One night,
after an hour of concentration, I became aware of myself as a
viewpoint located near the second chakra in the lower spinal
pathway. I saw my body's internal organs, circulatory system,

muscles, bones, nervous system, and brain illumined by radiant, white light and was able to observe with detached interest. After a while, I felt myself expand until I was again identified with my physical body.

I frequently saw visions of what seemed to be astral realms; Babaji, Lahiri Mahasaya, Sri Yukteswar, Master, and luminous beings unknown to me momentarily appeared in my spiritual eye. At times, my consciousness seemed to be so expanded that it included the cosmos. Some of these perceptions could have been mind-brain produced[3] phenomena.

Master had counseled me earlier: "Stay in tune with me and I will be able to help you. When you are restless or have doubts, it causes static in your mental radio that makes it more difficult for me to help you. So stay in tune with me."

While talking with a small group of disciples, he said, "When you are in tune with me, you can be in tune with God." I understood that he was telling us that, because he was always God-conscious, by attunement with him, we could also be aware of the reality of God.

During my first year of discipleship, occasional moods disturbed my inner peace as thoughts that liberation of consciousness might not soon occur passed through my mind. During one such temporary episode, Master mailed me a brief, handwritten note: "Dear Roy. You are making yourself unhappy by indulging in moods and playing a negative mental phonograph record in your mind. Why don't you break that record?" His practical words enabled me to discard the self-limiting habit.

I usually visited Master at his desert retreat, where two houses were on adjacent lots. He lived and worked in one of the houses; some of his female disciples who typed his letters and transcribed and edited his writings lived in the other house. Male disciples who did the maintenance work or who were visiting Master slept in a cottage a few miles distant.

During one of my visits to Twentynine Palms, while I was helping an older disciple fasten wire mesh to the wall of the garage to prepare it for plastering, Master walked by and stopped to chat. There was a small swimming pool a few feet from where he stood that had recently been installed for his use. Master asked the other disciple to get a pump from the garage and drain the pool so it could be cleaned.

The seemingly disinterested response was, "I can't do it now, Sir. I'm too busy with this job."

Turning to me, Master asked, "Roy, will you empty the pool?" Following his instructions, I found two five-gallon buckets and a short rope in the garage, and proceeded with the project.

Attaching the rope to one bucket, I took water from the pool, poured it into the second bucket, refilled the first one, and carried the water to some nearby shrubs. I soon discovered that a small swimming pool can contain many hundreds of gallons of water. By midafternoon, with sore hands and tired muscles, I was pleased to see that the water level in the pool had been significantly lowered.

The next morning, as I prepared to resume the task, Master came out of his house. From his vantage point near the patio, the pool appeared to be empty. "Look what Roy has done!" he exclaimed. When he came closer, he saw the water that remained in the pool. Without looking at the disciple who was working on the garage wall, he told him to get the pump and finish draining the pool.

Some of my most memorable occasions during those desert visits with Master were the early evening hours when he walked around the perimeter of the property and invited me to walk with him. If he noticed a scrap of paper on the ground, he would ask me to retrieve it. From time to time, when he saw a small stone, he would kick it a few feet ahead of him, as a child might do for amusement. Sometimes we walked in silence. At other times he talked about God and encouraged me to live a God-inspired life.

During one of our walks, he directed my attention to a nearby mountain. "Most people who see that mountain see only a mass of soil and rock," he said. "When I look at it, I see God."

After we had walked in silence for several minutes, he asked me if I had any questions.

I seldom went to Master with questions; just to be in his presence was sufficient. On that occasion, however, a question regarding some of the saints that he had written about in his autobiography surfaced in my mind.

"How many saints, who are mentioned in your book, are now fully liberated?" I inquired.

His response was immediate. "Not many. Many saints are so satisfied with the bliss of God-communion that they do not aspire to go beyond that stage."

After a pause, he said, "*You* must go all the way."[4]

During one of my early visits with him, a seemingly casual, yet transformative, incident occurred. Before going to Twentynine Palms I had experienced occasional pains in my chest and left arm, usually after a day of strenuous physical work.

While we were talking, he inquired, "How are your parents?" Before he finished speaking, misinterpreting his question as, "How is your pain?" I impulsively responded, "It's not too bad now, Sir."

With an expression of concern on his face, he asked, "What's not bad now?"

"This pain I've been having now and then," I told him.

"You have pain?" he inquired further.

As I began to try to describe the symptoms, he touched my chest with his hand, said, "You'll be all right now," and changed the theme of our conversation. The subject was not mentioned again. Nor did the symptoms return.

I had many opportunities to observe the various ways that Master beneficially influenced his disciples. His good manners and modes of behavior were exemplary. Always well-groomed, his body emanated a pleasant fragrance. To be in his presence was to be uplifted. During the course of a casual conversation, he would say something that would be meaningfully relevant to a person's need at that time. When a disciple misbehaved and direct confrontation was necessary, he did not hesitate to say what had to be said or do what had to be done to correct the situation. I know this from my personal experience.

While I was at the goat dairy in Scottsdale, Herbert sometimes asked me to make the milk deliveries when he was not able to do it because of his other duties. As I drove through the village of Scottsdale, I saw a bookstore and yielded to an impulse to stop there. While perusing a book in which the mystical experiences of a saint who had lived in India in the late 1800s were vividly described, I became fascinated. Knowing that Master had known the author and had spoken favorably about the saint, I purchased the book.

Feeling somewhat guilty because of remembering Master's admonition to me to read only his writings and a few other books that he recommended for the first year[5] that I was with him, I kept the book in my room where the other monks wouldn't see it, and privately read it each evening. While performing my duties each day, my mind was preoccupied with what I had read the night before, and my meditation sessions were not as focused as they had been.

A few weeks later, I visited SRF headquarters. When I arrived, Master's car was in the lower driveway. He was in the basement hallway talking with several disciples as he walked toward the car. He glanced in my direction but did not acknowledge me, as he had always done when I had been away for a while. I was standing next to him as he was about to get into the car. Without looking at me, he quietly announced to everyone, "Roy is a spiritual prostitute." He probably meant "adulterer"; the word he used made a stronger impact.

Without any explanation to the others, he looked at me. "There was a reason for why I told you to read only certain books during your first year. In another year or two, when your discrimination is more developed, you can read anything without being confused." After a moment of silence, he asked, "Are you all right, now?"

When I nodded my head, he said, "That's my boy."

Herbert later admitted that he had seen the book I had been reading and told Master about it.

Master did not approve of gossip; however, he did want to be informed about important matters. When Master would ask Herbert, "How is Roy?" Herbert would sometimes make what I considered to be a minor issue seem like a major problem.

In Phoenix, Herbert told me that he was going to ask the only wealthy member of our Center to donate money for two gallons of paint for one of the Center rooms. A few weeks later, when I asked him when I could begin the project, he said, "I haven't asked her yet. I'm waiting until I think she will be receptive to the idea."

A few weeks later, when Herbert went to California, I used some of my food allowance to buy the paint and complete the project. When he came back to Phoenix and saw what I had done, he was not pleased.

I visited Master at his retreat house a few weeks later. After talking with me for a while, he assumed a fatherly "Now, son, I have to discuss a serious matter with you, you naughty boy" demeanor, and said, "Herbert told me about the painting project. When are you going to learn to lose your self-will?" Then, smiling, he steered our conversation in another direction.

"Life has to be lived," he said, "why not live it the highest way? You could show me the most beautiful work of art and, if I wanted to, I could find some fault with it. But why should I do that? Always look for the good in everything."

On another occasion, knowing of my intense desire to be Self-realized, Master said, "You have to want God with such intense desire that you cannot wait another day to be God-realized, but you have to be patient if God is not realized that day."

I once experienced an episode of frustration, the cause of which I could not determine. I had every reason to be happy, but I wasn't, and I didn't know what to do to solve the problem. I telephoned Faye Wright and asked to talk with Master. She told me to go to the SRF Hermitage in Encinitas and that she would tell him that I had called.

The following evening, at the Encinitas Center, I went to the Hermitage. Leo Cocks,[6] a brother disciple, was with me. Master came into the room and sat on a couch. He talked briefly with Leo, then asked him to go into the other room.

He motioned for me to sit beside him and gently asked, "What's the matter?" Through a flood of tears that suddenly erupted, I said, "I don't know."

He put his arms around me, pulled me close, and held me as I cried on his shoulder. When the torrent of tears subsided, he asked, "Are you all right now?" I was.

He summoned Leo, told us who would take us to the bus station in San Diego, warmly blessed us, and sent us back to Phoenix that night.

During a visit to Twentynine Palms, the hour was late and the night was dark. I was with three brother disciples in front of Master's house when he came out to talk with us. A few women disciples were with him. After chatting for a few minutes, he directed a flashlight beam at my face and held it steady. Quietly, but loud enough for everyone to hear, he said, "When you first came to me, I asked the others (some of whom were present), 'Shall we keep him, or shall we let him go?' Do you know what they said?"

"No, Sir," I responded.

Master continued, "They said, 'He was sick before, and maybe he'll get sick again.' "

He paused. Everyone was silent for few moments.

"But I looked into your heart, and I said, 'He stays.' " After a short pause, he closed the conversation with, "Good night, Roy."

My guru could easily discern the karmic condition[7] of his disciples and of others whom he met. He would say, "I am not interested in having an organization for the sake of attracting a large membership. An organization such as ours is the hive; God is the honey. An organization without the honey of God is of little value. I am only interested in the welfare of souls."

As I became more conscious of subtle transformations that were occurring, I noticed how Master looked at disciples from time to time to discern their inner condition and degree of spiritual awareness. He looked at me that way when I visited him. If I had been meditating deeply and my mind was well-ordered, he would say, "Look how calm and God-loving you are becoming. Continue doing what you are doing." If I was not as soul-centered as I would have liked to have been, he would say, "Meditate more. Dive deep in the ocean of God. Pray to God. Tell him, 'Lord, I want nothing but you.' You will get there."

At times, when he would have to correct the behavior of disciples, he would also tell them, "I only do it because I want you to be as strong as I am."

To one young disciple who asked, "Why is my mind so restless?" Master replied, "Because you talk too much."

Master gave of himself to disciples in accord with their need and their capacity to receive his advice and his silent blessings. With me, he talked about God and the saints, of life's real purposes, and the importance of "one hundred percent" dedication to the spiritual path. He enlivened and unveiled my spiritual capacities, enriched my mind, and strengthened my faith.

Some of the disciples who worked closely with him were often challenged to keep up with his schedule of activities. He slept approximately three hours a night, often retiring to his room long after midnight. Sometimes, when talking with a disciple, or with a visitor who seemed receptive to learning, he would keep them with him until a new day dawned. Early every morning, he meditated for three or four hours before attending to organizational duties.

If someone expressed doubts about the possibility of his projects being successful or made negative comments about them, he would say, "People often tell me that what I am working on can't be accomplished. When the project is completed, everyone wants to be a part of it." When he decided to do something, he persisted. If anyone tried to discourage him, he might say, "God told me to do it!"[8] Of his many publishing and building projects, he said, "I always bite off more than I can chew, then I chew it."

While he was dictating a commentary on the Bhagavad Gita, a disciple who was present suggested that something he said should not be included in the book because some readers might disagree with it. Faye Wright later told me about the incident: "Master came out of his chair, paced the room like a lion, and demanded, 'Why can't we say that? It's true! I only speak the truth!'"

To a woman who expressed her surprise when Master seemed to be impatient with a monk who was working on a building project and spoke sharply to him, he remarked, "I am never angry; it's just that I have a fiery personality."

In 1950, the SRF Lake Shrine in Pacific Palisades was dedicated. Goodwin J. Knight, then the Lieutenant Governor of California, and other notable guests were introduced, a portion of Mahatma Gandhi's ashes was placed in a stone sarcophagus, and three disciples demonstrated yoga postures. As I observed the proceedings, I was preoccupied with a private matter.

A few days earlier, in Phoenix, as I was preparing to go to California to attend the opening of the Lake Shrine, I decided that when I talked with Master, I would ask him to give me a samadhi experience. The more I thought about it, the more certain I became that it would happen, and began to prepare myself by meditating deeply and practicing more kriya pranayamas, hoping to improve my receptivity.

During the overnight trip to California, I sat in the back row of the bus where I could be alone. Between short naps, I practiced kriya pranayama and meditated.

At the Lake Shrine, after the program was concluded, Master chatted amiably with a few friends and disciples. I waited until he was alone, and approached him. Touching his feet,[9] I asked, "Sir, will you give me samadhi?"

"What did you say?" he asked, obviously surprised.

When I repeated my request, he chuckled, grasped my forelock, turned to Mr. Lynn who was sitting beside him, and said, "He wants samadhi."

Mr. Lynn smiled, and murmured, "Bless his heart."

Several minutes later, while I was standing beside one of the golden lotus pillars, I saw Mr. Lynn walking along the nearby path that borders the lake. When I glanced at him, he came to where I stood. Without speaking, he put his left hand on my chest and his right hand on my head, and closed his eyes. I felt a fluid-like stream of energy flow into my body. I was momentarily breathless as waves of ecstasy permeated my body and my awareness expanded. Mr. Lynn then affectionately patted my shoulder and went to rejoin Master.

In 1951, when it became obvious that the goat dairy would not be as successful as had been earlier anticipated, it was sold, and I was transferred to the Phoenix Center. My duties were to clean the rooms, answer the telephone, prepare the chapel for the Sunday morning and Thursday evening services, and mow and water the lawn. After a few months, a Sunday evening discussion group was started and I was told to facilitate it. I also taught Hatha Yoga classes and occasionally demonstrated the postures at civic organizations and on local television.

I established a meditation routine which worked well for me. At three o'clock in the morning, I bathed and went into the chapel. After lighting a votive candle on the altar, I sat in a comfortable chair, chanted for several minutes, practiced meditation techniques, and sat in the silence. The morning session continued for four hours. A short session was scheduled at noon. Three hours each evening were also devoted to meditation practice.

When meditation did not flow easily, I prayed and chanted for a longer duration until my awareness was clear. Whether meditation was rewarding or not, I always sat for the chosen duration of time. Doing this was my personal commitment. Except for rare occasions when special activities required my attention or when I was asked by Master to visit him in California, this meditation routine was maintained for approximately two years.

I did not cultivate social relationships, nor did I read secular publications or have a radio or a television set. I read Master's books, the Bhagavad Gita, portions of the Bible, and biographies of several Catholic saints[10] which Master had recommended.

Devotional by nature, yet intent upon knowledge and realization of God, I always found my guru's instructions to be valid and practical. Inspired by his example and impelled by my own resolve, I adhered to my meditation schedules and holistic lifestyle practices.

An unusual event occurred during a Sunday afternoon meditation session. I had been sitting for about an hour when the sound of a door being forcefully closed interrupted my concentration. Herbert had started to come into the chapel, saw me, and hastily withdrew. Mildly disturbed, I closed my eyes and again turned my attention inward. Suddenly, I was a small viewpoint in a vast, blue space. My perception was spherical: I could see, simultaneously, in all directions. A multitude of distant, bright, white lights pervaded the seemingly infinite field of blue light. There was no sense of fear or strangeness.

Yoga literature provides information about a variety of states of consciousness which are accessible to one who is intent on discovering them. At the gaps between states of consciousness, and between thoughts that emerge and subside, it is possible to penetrate levels of consciousness that are more subtle. It can, therefore, be helpful to practice observing transitional states of consciousness: from sleep to wakefulness, from awake states to sleep, and when mental attitudes and mood changes occur during the day. With practice, the attentive observer of states of consciousness and mental states can learn to be always centered in Self-knowing.

After my initiation by Master in August, 1950, I received a special blessing from him. He began the initiation service by welcoming the resident disciples and visiting SRF students and said that during his early years in Boston, in the 1920s, when his classes were much smaller, he had more time to devote to each student and to help them see the light in the spiritual eye. He then explained how to practice kriya meditation techniques and invited everyone to come to where he sat to receive his blessings. As each person stood in front of him, he put his hand on their forehead. As he was blessing the people, I heard him say, "I am sending light into your body. I am giving you everything. It is up to you to receive it."

Immediately after the service, I helped some of my brother disciples remove the extra chairs. Master was sitting in a chair in front of the altar. Remembering his earlier comments about helping others to see the inner light, I went to him and asked him to help me see it.

Putting his hands on my forehead, he told me to look into the spiritual eye. Two brilliant, white lights in a dark blue field immediately appeared. As I gazed steadily into the spiritual eye, the two white lights began to merge. Before they came together, I was distracted by the sound of chairs being stacked, and the lights dispersed.

Master said, "Let's wait a moment." When he again put his hands on my forehead, the two white lights again appeared. He said, "Now, look into the distance." At that moment, the lights merged. As he removed his hands from my head, he said, "What you saw was Spirit and Nature. From now on, you can see that anytime."

When the two lights appeared, Master did not ask what I was seeing, nor did he offer advice until the critical moment when he said, "Look into the distance."

The light that can be seen when the mind is calm and attention is concentrated in the front and higher region of the brain is produced by the convergence of upward flowing currents of life force. The magnetic field that emanated from Master's hands, and his concentrated intention, had attracted my attention and life forces more strongly into the spiritual eye.

Master ordained me in 1951. I was at SRF headquarters with Herbert Freed, to attend a special late autumn function. The evening before the day we were to return to Phoenix, we encountered Master as he came into the basement entrance. He invited us to go with him to the upper level of the building.

After discussing matters regarding the Phoenix Center with Herbert, he asked me to kneel by his chair. With his hands on my head, he said, "I ordain you a minister of Self-Realization. Teach as I have taught. Heal as I have healed. Initiate devotees of God into Kriya Yoga."

Herbert, surprised by what Master had said, asked, "Sir, is

Roy to perform initiations?" Master's response was emphatic: "You, too. The same God who is in me, is in you. What I have done, you both should do."

My guru never claimed that what he taught originated with him. He always directed us to the Source, to God, and honored all authentic spiritual enlightenment traditions. I heard him say, "Disciples often argue about philosophical matters; enlightened masters understand each other and get along very well together."

On one occasion Herbert told him that a few people who attended services at the Phoenix Center had informed him that, while they enjoyed the midweek service, they wanted to go to a church on Sundays where their children could attend. At the time, the Phoenix Center did not have classes for children. Master advised, "Tell them to go to a Unity[11] Center."

To his disciples, Master would sometimes say, "I am not the guru. God is the guru. I am only his servant." On one occasion he said, "I banished Yogananda many years ago; only God dwells here[12] [in this body] now."

During one of our evening walks, in 1950, he told me, "You almost died last year, but your love for God pulled you through. You have a new life now; you must make the most of it." After a moment of reflection, in a tone of voice that indicated mild surprise as though an insight had just emerged into his awareness, he said, "You died young last time, too."

I asked him, "Sir, have I been with you before?"[13] He responded, "How could you be with me now if you had not been with me before? Of course, you have been with me before, and you will be with me many times in the future. You have come, as have some of the others, to help me with this work."

A disciple once asked Master, "Isn't Roy too new with us to be in Phoenix by himself?" Master admonished him, "Leave my boy alone. I know what I'm doing."

At SRF headquarters, in 1951, a brother disciple told me,

"Master wants to see you." I went to the main building and up the stairs to his room. Master, wearing pajamas, was sitting in his bed with the bedspread pulled up to his chest and his back supported by a large pillow. He invited me to sit in a chair next to him. He was relaxed and seemed to be very happy.

After a few minutes of conversation, he said, "Mr. Lynn is here for a few days. He has fulfilled all of my expectations for him. He is a good example for you and the others."

Master told me how the land above the Lake Shrine had been acquired. "Mr. Lynn and I were sitting together. I explained to him how important it was that we have that property to protect the privacy of the Lake Shrine. I asked him, 'Will you buy it for me?' I had never before talked to him like that. For the first time in our many years together, he wouldn't look at me. After a long time, he looked at me, with tears in his eyes, and said, 'Yes, Sir.' The last attachment that he had was attachment to money. I knew that, and chose that moment to help him get rid of it. He will be liberated in this lifetime."

Master then described how, in 1937, he had helped Mr. Lynn have his first transcendent samadhi experience, after Mr. Lynn had practiced meditation for five years.

"We were sitting on the beach at Encinitas. I looked at him and saw that he was ready. I put my hand on his chest and he instantly went into a deep samadhi state. He was not conscious of his body. His mouth had fallen open and I had to brush the flying insects away from his face. I let him be like that for a while before bringing him out of it."

As Master finished his narrative, Mr. Lynn, blissful and radiant, came into the room. Master told him, "I was just telling Roy about your first samadhi."

Mr. Lynn gently hugged Master, kissed his forehead, and quietly departed.

Guidelines for disciples at various SRF retreat centers were few. We were to be well-groomed, well-mannered, attend to our work duties, be considerate when engaged in personal interactions, and not become overly involved in personal relationships. We were to cultivate awareness of our true nature and of God's presence, and meditate on a regular schedule. Resident disciples were given five dollars a month for their personal use. When I was at the Phoenix Center, I was given a modest food and clothing allowance.

We did not attend formal classes; learning was experiential. Some newly ordained ministers worked with experienced ministers until they learned how to present classes and sermons. At other times, Master would tell a newly ordained disciple how to prepare a sermon.

To one ordained disciple he said, "Choose a theme that will be of interest. Write an outline of what you are going to talk about. Include a humorous story to illustrate a point and make everyone feel comfortable. Before speaking, review the outline, meditate deeply, then speak from your heart."

When he gave me similar advice, he told me to always lead a long meditation session at each Sunday or midweek service. "Dye them in the wool of Kriya Yoga practice," he advised. "That will be of greatest value."

He also told me to be sure that my shoes were shined, including the backs of the shoes, and to wear a robe when I counseled someone. "You are young," he said. "They will have more respect for you when they see you as a minister."

"If you have personal problems," Master told us, "don't talk about them with others and poison their minds. Come to me, or to someone to whom I send you for advice."

About training teachers and ministers, he said, "The most difficult thing for me has been to attract dedicated people who understand what we are doing and who will remain loyal to the teachings. Too often, they come here thinking that it will be easy;

or that they can learn a little, then teach what they think they know instead of what is real and important."

To me, and a few other young disciples, he counseled: "Prepare yourselves now. Today, thousands of people are seeking God. In the near future, millions will be seeking God and there will not be enough qualified teachers to meet the need. The world is undergoing difficulties now. Don't be concerned about them. Conditions will improve. In the future, yoga will be taught in schools and colleges.[14] You will see it happen. God's will, *will* be done, no matter what people do, or don't do. When you are in tune with God's will, you are carried along with it."

In November, 1951, while meditating, I had a vision of a group of people standing near a casket. The thought surfaced in my mind that I was seeing Master's funeral and I immediately telephoned Faye Wright and asked if he was all right. She assured me that he was well. I dismissed the vision as a product of my imagination.

A few days later, Herbert received a telephone call from Master, informing him that Sister Gyanamata,[15] an elderly disciple, had just died and that we were to come to Encinitas to attend her funeral service.

During the funeral service, Master told us of the events leading up to Sister Gyanamata's passing. She had been ill and was very weak. When Master was informed about her condition, he went to her room. When she asked for nirbikalpa (transcendent) samadhi, Master told her, "You don't need that. When you reach the palace, why do you want to go into the garden anymore?"

Sister Gyanamata understood the meaning of Master's words. He had often told a story about a man who was invited by a king to visit his palace. Arriving early at the palace gate, he was told to wait in a beautiful garden. Enthralled with what he saw, he forgot to keep his appointment with the king, and was not invited back to the palace. Master ended the story by saying, "If he had kept his appointment with the king and they became friends, he could have visited the garden anytime."

The "palace" represents transcendent God-realization; the "garden" represents subjective perceptions one might have when superconscious states are mixed with thoughts and emotions.

The next evening, when Master again went to see her, he said to her, "If you have any desire, I will fulfill it right now. You tell me." She replied, "No," three times. He then asked, "Is it true?" She replied, "Yes, Sir."

When Master left Sister Gyanamata's room, he asked Faye Wright and a few other disciples to go with him in his car and drive around in the Encinitas community. During the drive, he sat in meditative silence. After an hour, he said, "Now, let us go back." At the Hermitage, when he was told that Sister Gyanamata had just left her body, he went into her room alone for a few minutes, then asked Faye Wright and the other disciples to come into the room to feel the top of her head, which was hot. He explained that this indicated that she had left her body in the highest state of samadhi, departing through the crown chakra. He then told them that he, too, would soon be leaving this world, which he did less than four months later. Master had told a few disciples, "I will not long outlive Sister."

I was with Master, in Twentynine Palms, a few weeks before he left his body.

We were sitting in the living room of his house. He was relaxing in a large reclining chair. Virginia Wright brought him a small glass of pineapple juice, and waited until he drank it.

As she left the room, he said, "For years, I have not given much attention to my body. Now, as you have seen, they make me do it. Take care of your body, Roy. You have much work to do."

He was vital and radiantly blissful. "I just finished the last chapter of the Bhagavad Gita[16] [commentary]," he told me. "A little while ago, I was sitting here, meditating. I saw a ball of gold light in the spiritual eye. When I opened my eyes, I still saw it, *there."* He pointed to a place on the wall. "Babaji, Lahiri Mahasaya, and Sri Yukteswar appeared in the light. They were smiling. They came to thank me. They are pleased with me." He was almost childlike as he spoke, obviously happy to have completed an important project.

Leaning close, he said, "Don't allow yourself to be too concerned about what others do or don't do. Don't look back. Don't look to the left or to the right. Look straight ahead to the goal, and go all the way in this lifetime. You can do it. Sri Yukteswar used to say, 'The boat that carries souls across the river of delusion is ready to depart. Who will go? Who will go? If no one goes, I will go.' You must be like that!"

He talked more about his guru: "Before Sri Yukteswar passed, once, while we were talking, his body suddenly trembled. When I expressed my concern, he said, 'Just as a caged bird may be hesitant to leave its cage and be free, sometimes the soul is reluctant to leave the body and experience omnipresence.' "

Looking at me, Master asked, "Do you understand?" I felt that he was preparing me for his own soon departure.

A few months earlier, he told me, and other disciples, that he was "living on borrowed time" and had only a few more duties to fulfill and a few more disciples to meet. He said that his mission had been to establish yoga teachings in the West and to assist certain disciples, whom he said would be attracted to him, to Self- and God-realization.

Before concluding our session, he took a twenty dollar bill from the side pocket of his trousers, folded it, and put it into my shirt pocket. "Use this for food," he said. "You must stay strong and healthy to do the work you have to do."

CHAPTER THREE NOTES

1. Herbert Freed (circa 1929 – 1994) was the resident minister at the SRF Center in Phoenix from 1949 to 1952. After two years of service in the U.S. Army (1954-56) he formed a small-business consulting firm in Florida and was later a juvenile parole officer in Los Angeles where he and his wife also provided homes for disadvantaged teenage children.

2. The Self-Realization Fellowship Temple in Phoenix, Arizona, is at 6111 North Central Avenue. The first SRF Center in Phoenix, at 1800 West Monroe Street, was dedicated by Paramahansa Yogananda in 1948.

3. Recent studies by neuroscientists during which brain scans were used to determine which parts of the brain are either active or passive when meditators experience a calm, tranquil state indicate that the prefrontal lobes of the brain are usually involved. When one meditator reported that he experienced a sense of boundless freedom from time and space, a brain scan indicated that the centers in the back, upper hemispheres of his brain that process sensory input had been passive during that interval of meditation. In experiments during which a mild magnetic field was applied to the left temporal region of the brain, some subjects said they "felt" an invisible "presence" in the room, which ceased to exist when the magnetic field was turned off. Prior to undergoing a surgical procedure, a woman whose back, right region of the brain was stimulated with a mild electric current, reported a sensation of being out of her body.

A meditator should learn to discern the difference between mind-brain produced phenomena and experiences that are the result of authentic spiritual awakening.

Some scientists used to believe that the connections between brain cells were fixed early in life and did not later change. It is now known that meditation can change the circuitry of the brain. Paramahansa Yogananda often said that the brain could be developed by meditation, kriya pranayama practice, and intentional, creative use of the mind.

4. Paramahansaji's advice to me to aspire to be fully liberated rather than be satisfied with sustained enjoyment of meditative states is in accord with the teachings in Patanjali's yoga-sutras.

5. My guru's advice that I read only specific writings during my first year with him was for the purpose of enabling me to be in mental and spiritual attunement with him, and to acquire basic, useful information and apply it. Thus, his instruction to me during our first conversation to read a little, meditate more, and to think of God all of the time. By reading the book that I had purchased at the Scottsdale bookstore during my first year with him, I had adulterated (mixed and rendered somewhat impure) the thoughts in my mind and my attunement with him. Later, as he told me, I could read more widely and easily discern what was of value for me.

6. Leo Cocks (Sept. 8, 1929 –) became a member of the SRF monastic order in 1950 and worked with me at the goat dairy in Scottsdale, Arizona, for several months. Shortly after our guru's mahasamadhi, he moved to San Francisco, worked for several years, and continued his spiritual practices. After he and his wife retired, they moved to Encinitas, California.

7. Karma is a word used to indicate causative influences, such as habitual thoughts, intentions, desires, cravings, our tendencies to react to events and circumstances instead of to rationally respond, and the accumulation of memories and subconscious impressions that influence (or have potential to influence) thoughts, moods, and behaviors. As long as we are affected by such influences we are not truly Self-determined. Our thoughts, moods, behaviors, and states of consciousness should be wisely regulated. What we intend to experience or accomplish should be wisely chosen. All desires should be monitored to determine which desires are of value. Unwholesome cravings should be renounced. We should respond constructively and appropriately to events that occur and circumstances that arise. Memories should be viewed as mere impressions of past perceptions. The influences of subconscious impressions that are troublesome should be neutralized. False beliefs and illusions should be renounced. An effective way to resist, weaken, and eliminate subconscious influences is to assume mental attitudes, feelings, and states of consciousness that are more life-enhancing and to implement behaviors that are constructive. Superconscious influences effectively resist, weaken, and neutralize the influences of troublesome karma.

8. When Paramahansa Yogananda said, "God told me to do it," he meant that he was inspired to do it.

9. In India, and in some other regions of Asia, touching someone's feet is commonly done as a gesture of respect.

10. Paramahansaji occasionally recommended that his monastic disciples read about some of the Catholic mystics because of their devotion, discipline, and commitment to spiritual practice. He often spoke favorably about Saint Theresa of Avila, Saint John of the Cross, Saint Francis, and Saint Anthony.

11. The Unity movement, started by Charles Fillmore and his wife, Myrtle, in 1889, promoted a wholesome, metaphysical approach to living with emphasis on meditation, prayer, healing, and a vegetarian diet. Truth seekers in many countries of the world derive benefit by attending Unity church services and reading its publications. *The Daily Word* magazine has a readership far exceeding the organization's membership. A book, *The Unity Movement* (by Neal Vahle, Templeton Foundation Press) is a comprehensive source of information.

12. When Paramahansaji sometimes said, "Only God dwells in this body now," he was not implying that he was an avatar—an incarnation of God in human form. Some of his disciples prefer to believe that he was a divine incarnation and are forthright in promoting their opinion. While he did express divine attributes, he described in *Autobiography of a Yogi* his need, during his early years, to learn from others.

13. Many people presume reincarnation to be a fact without having actual knowledge about it. One of the most reliable indications that souls can reincarnate may be that many spiritually awake people declare that it can occur. Paramahansa Yogananda often mentioned reincarnation, emphasizing that what is done now to awaken to Self-realization is more important than what may have occurred before.

14. Paramahansaji's comments regarding yoga eventually being taught in schools and colleges have come true. Meditation and Hatha Yoga are now taught in several private schools, and in some medical schools, hospitals, and clinics as ways to manage stress, slow biologic aging processes, and strengthen the body's immune system.

15. Sister Gyanamata (Edith Ann Bissett, 1869 – 1951) was living in Seattle, Washington, with her husband and son when she met Paramahansa Yogananda, in 1925. In 1932, after her husband, Clark Bissett, a professor of the University of Washington Law School, died, she moved to the SRF headquarters in Los Angeles and, later, lived at the Hermitage in Encinitas for the rest of her life. Quietly, selflessly dedicated to serving others, she inspired everyone who knew her. Paramahansaji said that, though she practiced yoga, her path was that of knowledge-wisdom, and that her spiritual liberation occurred by grace.

16. The Bhagavad Gita has spiritually nurtured millions of people for more than two thousand years. The two central characters in the fictional story are Arjuna and Krishna. Arjuna represents the true seeker of knowledge and experience of God. Krishna represents one's illumined consciousness. In eighteen chapters, a broad range of philosophical concepts are fully explored and practical advice about how to live skillfully and effectively is provided. Many readers presume the text to affirm that Krishna is God in human form; an insightful examination reveals that what is described is a formless, transcendent Reality that is to be realized. In the first ten chapters, the ways of knowledge (Jnana Yoga), meditation (Raja Yoga), devotional love (Bhakti Yoga), and right, selfless actions (Karma Yoga) are described. In the eleventh chapter, Arjuna is enabled, by grace, to perceive supreme Consciousness as all things. The concluding chapters are devoted to explanations of how to use what has been learned.

CHAPTER FOUR

Transitions

On March 7, 1952, Herbert telephoned me late in the evening from Los Angeles to tell me that Master had just made his transition. He provided a few details and told me to conduct a memorial service for Master at the Phoenix Center before going to Los Angeles.

At SRF headquarters, Master's body, dressed in one of his ochre robes, was on his bed. Several disciples stood nearby. I was saddened to know that Master would not open his eyes and smile in recognition and welcome. Yet, I was not desolate. He had prepared me for this event and my attunement with his spirit remained. What I would miss was his vibrant voice, the touch of his hand in blessing, and those special occasions of intimacy.

On March 11, all of the resident disciples and many SRF members from far and near gathered for the two-hour, late afternoon memorial service for Master at SRF headquarters. His body, in a bronze casket,[1] was in front of the altar in the chapel. Doctor Lewis read from the New Testament and the Bhagavad Gita. Mr. Lynn spoke for a few moments, as did Oliver Black,[2] a long-time disciple and the SRF minister in Detroit, Michigan. Mr. Binay Ranjan Sen, India's Ambassador to the United States, delivered a eulogy during which he mentioned that, as he was being driven to the summit of Mt. Washington, he had seen a rainbow, which he felt was an auspicious sign.

At the conclusion of the service, we walked slowly by the casket to view Master's countenance for the final time, dropping rose petals on the glass covering while chanting, "Om guru, Om guru." His body was then taken to Forest Lawn Memorial-Park[3] in nearby Glendale, California.

I sought a secluded place behind the main building, to be alone, after which I encountered Oliver Black, who shared private words of comfort and understanding.

We had observed Master's fifty-ninth birthday with him just two months before his passing. At that time he shared his hopes for our spiritual growth and publicly announced that his Bhagavad Gita commentary had been completed.

On March 4, Master hosted Ambassador Sen, Mrs. Sen, and a few others at a private dinner at SRF headquarters, and had private talks with some disciples. On March 6, he was driven to the Pacific Palisades Lake Shrine. There, he walked around the lake, had lunch with some disciples, played the organ in the chapel, and repeatedly chanted words written by the Indian poet Rabindranath Tagore: "In my house with Thine own hands, light the lamp of Thy love." He then returned to SRF headquarters.

Herbert rode in the car with Master and later told me that he had been enthusiastic about a new project. "I have an opportunity to start another work in the midwest, very similar to this one, which will not interfere with what we are doing here," he said. He did not elaborate; he may have been referring to a project that he had already discussed with Oliver Black regarding the establishment of a retreat center in northern Michigan.

On March 7, Master stayed in his room in meditative silence until going, late that afternoon, to the Biltmore Hotel in downtown Los Angeles where a room had been reserved for him. As he prepared to depart from SRF headquarters, he commented to a few disciples, "Imagine! I have a room at the Biltmore! I'm going back to where it all started." He was referring to when he stayed there for several weeks, in 1925, when he lectured to many thousands of people in the nearby Philharmonic Auditorium.

That evening, Master was at a banquet sponsored by The

Indian Association of America to honor Ambassador Sen. More than two hundred guests attended the event. When Master was introduced, before he stood up to go to the microphone, he said to Mrs. Sharma, one of the guests who was seated beside him, "Always remember that life has its beautiful roses and it also has its thorns, and we must accept both."

During his short talk, he spoke more slowly than he usually did, about his ideal of peaceful cooperation between nations of the world, and concluded his ten minute talk at 9:30 p.m. by reciting a portion of one of his poems, "My India." As he finished the last sentence—"I am hallowed; my body touched that sod"— he raised his eyes, turned slightly to the right, and slumped to the floor. Faye Wright, and several other disciples, rushed forward to assist him, but he had gone.

Herbert told me what he had observed that evening: "When Master was speaking, now and then his eyes were pulled up to his spiritual eye and he had to use his power of will to keep his attention focused on his talk."

Mr. Lynn was at the Encinitas Hermitage when Master made his transition in Los Angeles. When I was informed of this, I remembered what Master had said a few weeks before, at a gathering of disciples. He told us that once, during a deep meditation, he expanded beyond his body and was rejoicing in that freedom. A disciple who went into his room noticed that he was not breathing and quickly summoned Mr. Lynn, who was in the building. Mr. Lynn sat by Master, meditated, and mentally asked him to return to physical awareness, which he did. While telling us about the experience, Master said, "I wasn't going to come back. The next time I go, I'll make sure Mr. Lynn isn't nearby."

Two months after Master left his body, the directors of the Forest Lawn Memorial-Park Association sent a letter to Self-Realization Fellowship in which the first paragraph provided the following information:

The absence of any signs of decay in the body of Paramahansa Yogananda offers the most extraordinary case in our experience. Had the muscle protein and bloodstream of the deceased not been comparatively free of bacteria, deterioration of the body could have set in as early as six hours after life had departed. No physical disintegration was visible in Paramahansa Yogananda's body even twenty days after death.

Master's body had not been immediately placed in a crypt because it was expected that some members of Yogoda Satsanga, the Indian branch of Self-Realization Fellowship, would be coming to America to view it.

During the last two years of his life, Master experienced episodes of physical discomfort. When India House, adjacent to the Hollywood SRF church, was dedicated, I was asked to be at the side entrance with three of my brother disciples when Master arrived, and to help him go down the narrow stairs to the lower level fellowship hall. Even though he seemed to be tired and it was painful for him to walk, he was very happy because a new, worthwhile project had been completed.

One cause of his short-term physical discomfort may have been overwork, which is characteristic of many people who are strongly mission-oriented, as he was. He slept very little, attended to organizational details, and often worked long hours writing, dictating letters, and talking with disciples. He was also concerned about the future of "the work," as he referred to the organization. It is believed by some disciples that he absorbed the physical karma of others to ease their suffering. He said that he had done this for some people.

The transfer of subtle causes of physical disabilities from a person who is being helped to the person who is helping may occur when a sympathetic attunement is established at causal and astral levels. This method of helping is not recommended for the ordinary person.

It must also be said that some disciples of an enlightened teacher do not want to believe that their teacher has personal karma, inherited genetic predispositions for illness, or may have a physical disability because of stress or other causes. It is more convenient for them to believe that their teacher has taken on the karma of others, or of planetary conditions, and to endeavor to encourage others to accept their opinions.

To disciples who had asked Master about their attunement with him when he was no longer in the body, he said, "If you think me near, I will be near." To me he had said, "Whenever you initiate anyone into Kriya Yoga, I, or one of the gurus, will be there."[4]

The organization had disciples who were trained to teach and to disseminate his writings. He had also authorized a few ordained disciples to initiate their students without having to be supervised by the SRF Board of Directors. He knew that the transmission and empowerment of Kriya Yoga teachings through the lineage of gurus would continue through his spiritually advanced disciples and their successors.

Self-Realization Fellowship later announced to its members that Paramahansa Yogananda was the last in the lineage of SRF gurus. This statement is mistakenly believed by many people to mean that he was the last guru in the lineage; that he had no guru-successors.[5] It was also stated that those who were initiated in the future by a minister of the organization were to accept Paramahansa Yogananda as their guru. Thousands of people who were initiated since 1952, who were told to accept him as their guru, do not have a teacher who is accessible for instruction and guidance. They may be inspired by Master's writings, feel uplifted when they think of him, or imagine that they are in tune with him, but they cannot be instructed or guided by him.

At one of his last meetings with the Board of Directors of Self-Realization Fellowship, Master said that, through the years, he had always generously offered initiation to students who attended his classes and subscribed to the printed lessons. He explained that many of them had not maintained their affiliation with him or the organization after being initiated because they thought that they had received all that was offered. He then recommended that, in the future, every person who requested initiation should be made aware of the value of maintaining their affiliation so they could have support and encouragement on their spiritual path when it was most needed.

At the 1951 kriya initiation, Master announced that Mr. Lynn would be the next spiritual director and president of Self-Realization Fellowship, and gave him the name Rajasi Janakananda. His choice of the word *Rajasi* was intended to mean "royal rishi (seer)." *Janakananda*, "bliss (ananda) like that of Janaka's" was chosen to compare Mr. Lynn's state of God-realization with a saint-like king of ancient India. A few years later, some disciples discussed Master's choice of the word and decided that it should have been *Rajarsi*. On my SRF Teacher Certificate, dated March 9, 1952, Mr. Lynn signed his name as Rajasi Janakananda.

Shortly after Master's mahasamadhi, Mr. Lynn, while with a gathering of his brother and sister disciples, assured them that he would not ask for any drastic changes to be made in organizational operations and said, "Master will always be our guru. There will never be another guru for Self-Realization Fellowship." It was, therefore, presumed that Master's written and recorded words would fulfill the needs of future students and that all present and future ministers of the organization would represent him rather than be teachers in the lineage of gurus.

During informal talks, Master had said that some of his disciples (he mentioned Oliver Black, Sister Gyanamata, and one or two others) had disciples. While he wanted the organization that he founded to promulgate his teachings far into the future, he also knew that the spiritual force that flows through the lineage of gurus would continue to be transmitted through some of his disciple-successors.

The day after Master's memorial service, Faye Wright informed me that he had earlier told her that I was to be the minister in Phoenix. Herbert was transferred to California.

In Phoenix, I conducted the Sunday morning and Thursday evening services and maintained a schedule of early morning and evening meditation practice.

During the summer of 1953, I began to ponder the idea of withdrawing from monastic life. Though my devotion to God was constant, I felt a need to have experience in the secular world. After much soul-searching, I met with Faye Wright to discuss the matter. We talked about the possibility of my moving to another city where, after I was settled and self-sufficient, I might establish an SRF-affiliated meditation group. Until I was certain that I had made the right decision, however, I was to remain at the Phoenix Center.

A few months later, with Master's words—"You have a wonderful future"—echoing in my mind and my heart, and being receptive to all of the good fortune that God's grace could provide, I chose a new course for my life.

When I telephoned Faye Wright, in Los Angeles, and Mr. Lynn, in Kansas City, and told them what I had decided, they were empathetic. Mr. Lynn wistfully said, "I wish you had talked with me about this."

Uncertain about what to do, I enlisted in the Army and served for two years in the medical corps. In 1955, at Fort Riley, Kansas, with a few months of military service yet to be completed, I made what I thought were practical plans. I would go to a Chiropractic college, have a successful practice in Denver, Colorado, which would be of service to others, establish a meditation center, and continue to teach in affiliation with Self-Realization Fellowship. I was soon to discover, however, that one's personal plans are not always in accord with the trends of future events.

In late February of that year, a young man with whom I worked in the hospital at Fort Riley and to whom I had taught meditation practices, handed me the morning edition of a Kansas City newspaper that featured a front-page article announcing the death of James Lynn. Surprised by the news, I did not then know that his absence might influence my choices of future ministry endeavors.

Before returning to civilian life, I mailed a letter to Faye Wright, who had been newly chosen as the president of SRF, in which I described my plan to go to Denver and my readiness to establish a meditation center. Her responsive letter informed me that the Board of Directors had decided that I should not be permitted to do it. My first reaction elicited mild feelings of disappointment and of having been rejected. A few days later, after objectively analyzing their decision, I realized that it was the right one, for them and for me.

Master had provided the SRF Board of Directors with guidelines regarding the publication and distribution of his writings, the establishment of new temples, and training of monastics, ministers, and teachers. He told them to regularly advertise *Autobiography of a Yogi* in magazines which had a large readership and to expand the organization's influence in the world. It was their duty to follow his instructions to the best of their ability, which they have done. Mr. Lynn's passing occurred three years after Master left his body, and the Board of Directors had to make decisions that could have far-reaching effects. I had to grow to emotional and spiritual maturity and be free to do the work that I had to do.

In Denver, I rented a lecture hall, presented a series of public lectures, conducted meditation classes twice a week for a year, initiated several people, and began to publish a newsletter and a quarterly magazine. I also outlined, and announced, a detailed plan to build a Shrine of All Faiths retreat center near Denver which would have a meditation temple, classrooms, guest houses, a library, a health spa, and a publishing department. I naively presumed that when the project was publicized, enthusiastic cooperation and generous funding would be immediately forthcoming. Several people said it was a good idea; no one offered to participate. I did not then know that my project was premature or that, sixteen years later, unplanned events would occur to make possible its fulfillment, not in Colorado, but in northeast Georgia, in the foothills of the Appalachian Mountains.

Knowing that the ministry to which I was called would eventually be international in scope, I decided to travel and teach in other cities in the United States.

CHAPTER FOUR NOTES

1. The physical body of a swami is not (usually) cremated because it is considered to have been symbolically burned when worldly attachments were renounced.

2. Oliver Black (1893 – 1989) was born in Grover Hills, Ohio, and grew up in Indiana. In 1920, in Detroit, Michigan, starting with $500 he formed Peninsular Metal Products which manufactured automobile parts and eventually became a multimillion dollar publicly held company. He met Paramahansa Yogananda in Detroit in 1931, became a disciple, was soon ordained, conducted Sunday and midweek services for many years, and initiated hundreds of people into Kriya Yoga meditation practices. After retiring from his business activities in 1967, he founded Song of the Morning Ranch: A Yoga Retreat of Excellence on 800 acres of wooded land near Vanderbilt, Michigan. In 1976, six years after his wife died, he moved to the retreat, supervised its development, and conducted classes until his passing at the age of ninety-six.

During his final years, though physically frail, he was active and mentally alert. While at the Ostego Memorial Hospital in Gaylord, Michigan, after having a physical examination he was assigned a private room. Late the next day, with several of his disciples present, sitting on his bed in a meditative mood, he consciously left his body.

Mr. Black, who was given the title of Yogacharya (one who lives a God-directed life) by Paramahansa Yogananda, had a warm, outgoing personality and a direct manner of speaking and acting. At a memorial service that was conducted at Song of the Morning Ranch by SRF minister Sister Mukti Mata who came from Los Angeles, one of Mr. Black's disciples told of his influence on her and others whom he had guided: "He accepted us as we were and encouraged us to discover and bring out our full potential. Many of us didn't know how to love or to how to trust—he taught us to love and to trust. He gave us what many of us had never had, a safe place to be, and a never-failing divine friendship. He taught us to meditate, and to love God."

Mr. Black's brother and sister disciples enjoyed hearing about his experiences with Paramahansaji. He told us that our guru had telephoned him from California, asked him to initiate three men who would be visiting Detroit, and said "I will be with you when you do it." While Mr. Black was meditating with the men, he heard a vibration in the room and briefly saw Paramahansaji standing before him. When I asked if the other men had seen Master, he said, "No, but they all felt his presence, and one of them shed tears of devotion." As Mr. Black entered his home later that evening, the telephone was ringing. When he picked it up, Paramahansaji said, "See, Oliver, I told you I'd be with you!"

3. Paramahansa Yogananda's crypt in The Hall of Golden Slumbers, in Holly Terrace of the Great Mausoleum, at Forest Lawn in Glendale, California, is a pilgrimage site that is frequently visited by many Kriya Yoga adherents.

4. When my guru told me, "Whenever you initiate anyone into Kriya Yoga, I, or one of the gurus, will be there," he meant that the consciousness and spiritual force of one or more of the lineage of gurus would be present; not that they would always actually be there.

5. Because the few living disciples of Paramahansaji who serve as ministers or counselors, or conduct initiations, consider themselves to be his representatives rather than teachers, I am his only remaining guru-successor.

CHAPTER FIVE

Continuing Grace

From late 1957 until the early 1970s I lectured[1] and presented meditation seminars in more than fifty cities in North America, initiated hundreds of truth seekers, spoke at yoga conferences, was interviewed on regional and national radio and television talk shows, and wrote several books.

Inspired and highly self-motivated, I soon learned that the events or circumstances I imagined, and believed to be possible, would almost effortlessly occur. I was thus able to experience what spiritually enlightened people have taught through the ages: an enlivening, intelligently directed Power nurtures the universe and we can learn to cooperate with its inclinations to be supportively expressive. When we do, we become increasingly aware of an invisible Reality that provides for our every need when we learn to rely on It.

In 1971, the unplanned events that would culminate in the establishment of a retreat center began to unfold. After one of my lectures in Atlanta, Edwin and Lois O'Neal invited me to join them for a late supper. They informed me about the work they were doing in northeast Georgia, where they had purchased ten acres of wooded property in Lakemont, near Lake Rabun, for a spiritual community. To fund the project, they had formed a commercial printing business that soon evolved into a book publishing company. When they asked for permission to publish and distribute my books, I agreed to their proposal. In 1972, they invited me to be a permanent member of their Board of Directors and to be responsible for ministry activities on my own terms.

I moved to Lakemont in 1973, organized office procedures to coordinate Center for Spiritual Awareness[2] activities, outlined plans for the development of our retreat center, and continued to travel and lecture several months each year. Lois died in 1976, after a short illness. Two years later, Edwin resigned, and I was appointed as the president of our nonprofit corporation. Because the printing business had not been profitable, I closed it in order to focus my attention entirely on ministry activities.

Development of the retreat facilities proceeded smoothly. A meditation hall, dedicated in 1977; six guest houses; library buildings; the Shrine of All Faiths Meditation Temple; and a book store were built during the following ten years. Building projects and ministry services are primarily funded by the donations of our members, who live in many countries of the world and are sent monthly printed lessons by mail.

Weekend and week long retreats are scheduled here from early spring until late autumn. In early spring, I usually go to a few cities in North America, and sometimes to Europe, India, and West Africa to present seminars and initiate prepared persons into Kriya Yoga meditation practices.

The mission-purpose of Center for Spiritual Awareness is to use every available means to provide helpful information to sincere truth seekers everywhere and to encourage them to experience their highest good in all aspects of their lives as they progressively awaken to Self- and God-realization.

Human nature is the same in all parts of the world. Every person, consciously or unconsciously, yearns to know their true nature and their relationship with the Infinite. During occasions of undisturbed aloneness, when external events are ignored and no longer impress our senses, we can intuitively know that our sojourn in this world is but a brief interlude in space-time, and that our innate urge to have our awareness restored to its original, pure wholeness cannot continue to be denied or ignored.

Self-realization can definitely be accomplished by every reasonably intelligent person who chooses to live a well-ordered life and to nurture their spiritual growth. Their awakening will then progress from ordinary, egocentric states of consciousness to superconsciousness, cosmic consciousness, Self-realization, and God-realization. The culmination of right endeavor is complete, permanent liberation of consciousness.

The side-benefits of spiritual practice—improved physical health, peace of mind, harmonious relationships, comfortable circumstances, and the ability to live more effectively—can be appreciated. It should be remembered, however, that the ultimate purpose for spiritual practice is to be Self-realized.

The spiritual path is the way of aloneness in God. Outer, wholesome, supportive relationships can be maintained and meaningful purposes can be accomplished while one remains anchored in Self-knowing and God-awareness. While it can be of value to acknowledge the spiritual status of others who are already Self-realized, and to associate with them when possible, every person must awaken to their own realization of their true nature and their relationship to God.

Through the years it has been my experience that, while I have endeavored to wisely use my acquired knowledge and skills, most of the favorable events that have occurred in my life have been provided by God's grace—which I acknowledge, and for which I am thankful.

CHAPTER FIVE NOTES

1. In 1964 and 1978 I lectured in several cities in Japan for Seicho-No-Ie, a truth movement with two million members founded in 1931 by Dr. Masaharu Taniguchi. During the past three decades I have frequently lectured, presented meditation seminars, and conducted Kriya Yoga initiation services throughout North America and in Germany, Switzerland, Italy, England, West Africa, Brazil, and India.

2. The name of the nonprofit corporation that was formed by Mr. and Mrs. O'Neal in 1964 was Christian Spiritual Alliance, chosen because it was innocuous and the acronym CSA could be used to designate it and Cool Spring Acres—the name by which the retreat site was known when it was purchased. I named the ministry outreach department *Center for Spiritual Awareness* to more accurately distinguish our ideals and purposes. CSA Press is our book and literature publishing department.

A free information packet, a book list, and meditation retreat and seminar schedules can be obtained from our office.

Center for Spiritual Awareness
P.O. Box 7
Lakemont, Georgia 30552-0001
Telephone 706-782-4723
Fax 706-782-4560
e-mail: csainc@csa-davis.org
web site: www.csa-davis.org

CHAPTER SIX

Answers to Questions

What did Paramahansa Yogananda do for recreation and for enjoyment?

He seemed to be most happy when he was with sincere truth seekers or creatively engaged in worthwhile projects. At large public gatherings he would say, "I prefer a God-loving soul to a crowd, but I love to be with crowds of God-loving souls."

During his early years, he played tennis and table-tennis, walked, hiked, and enjoyed swimming, boating, open spaces, oceans, lakes, forests, and mountains. He liked the SRF centers to be beautifully landscaped and to have a variety of flowers, shrubs, and trees. His food preparation skills were well-developed and often innovative. If he discovered a new recipe that intrigued him, he experimented with it until the results satisfied him and pleased the palates of his guests. Movies were infrequently attended. In early 1950, when Uday Shankar was in southern California with his classical Indian dance troupe, Master hosted a lunch for them at the Encinitas Hermitage and attended their evening performance in Los Angeles, which he later said was flawless. For rest and renewal, he occasionally went to the Encinitas SRF center by the ocean or to his desert retreat in Twentynine Palms, to be in seclusion and devote more time to prolonged meditation.

Did Paramahansa Yogananda express feelings of sadness, anger, or hostility?

He was temporarily sad when someone who was close to him

died, when others suffered, or when a disciple who could have been Self-realized strayed from the spiritual path. He was never angry. His compassion for others was limitless.

Did your guru ever make any dire predictions?

He said that there would be regional and global conflicts, economic difficulties, and some natural disasters that would occur. Knowing the trends of evolution and the transformative changes occurring in the collective consciousness of the planet (see *yuga* in the Glossary), he was optimistic in actively promoting his vision of peace and harmony for all people in a world without war, poverty, or narrow religious sectarianism.

In his writings, Paramahansa Yogananda sometimes referred to God as a Heavenly Father, Divine Mother, Him, Her, He, She, and in other ways that denote a personalized concept of God. At other times, his emphasis was more absolute. Why did he do this?

How he spoke or wrote about God was determined by whether his mood was devotional or more elevated, and by the state of consciousness and ability to comprehend of those to whom he was speaking or writing. Wanting to communicate his message to everyone, he chose words that might satisfy a variety of needs. Regarding his mission, he emphasized what he called the *quantity* work and the *quality* work. *Quantity* work was for the purpose of teaching as many people as possible in all walks of life the basic lifestyle guidelines and spiritual practices that could be helpful to them. *Quality* work could be done with disciples who had the intellectual capacity to understand the real value of what he taught and who would diligently apply it. To me, he emphasized the ideal of realizing the formless, nameless aspect of God.

Paramahansaji's quantity work attracted criticism from a few yoga teachers in India who expressed their opinion that he had

diluted the teachings to make them acceptable to people in the
West. He taught the practices of yoga in ways that people could
understand them. Some of his critics also said (and say) that he
taught kriya meditation techniques in a simplistic way to make
it easier for his Western students to practice them. A few years
ago, I was talking with a swami from India who said this. When
I informed him that Paramahansaji had taught all of the intri-
cate meditation practices, he said, "Oh, I didn't know that." The
swami had been listening to gossip; he had not talked with anyone who had personal knowledge of what my guru taught.

Why did Paramahansa Yogananda quote from the Bible, write
commentaries on it, and endeavor to favorably compare some
Christian doctrines with yoga practices?

When he came to America in 1920, and through the years
that followed, to assure the people who attended his lectures that
he was not going to ask them to forsake their Christian heritage,
he often quoted verses from the Bible that could be interpreted
as being compatible with yoga practices. He also wrote commentaries on the New Testament that were published for many years
in *Self-Realization* magazine. His commentaries were edited and
published in 2004.

When I heard him talk at group gatherings, he sometimes
quoted Bible verses and remarked that Jesus had practiced yoga
meditation methods in India. When I was privately with him, he
did not talk to me about these matters. His endeavors to relate
Christian concepts to Kriya Yoga practices was a way to reach a
broader audience, an aspect of his quantity work.

Paramahansaji encouraged people to be universal in their
outlook and to respect all useful modes of spiritual practice. The
name that he chose for the SRF temples in Hollywood and San
Diego in the early 1940s was Self-Realization Church of All Religions, to let people know that the underlying truth in all mean-

ingful religious traditions was acknowledged and honored there. In his early writings, he recommended that people occasionally visit various Christian churches, Synagogues, Mosques, and Buddhist and Hindu temples, and to appreciate the religious views and practices of others.

Just as Lahiri Mahasaya and Sri Yukteswar taught Kriya Yoga practices to adherents of any religious faith, so my guru welcomed everyone and related to them in ways that were compatible with their religious views, psychological temperament, capacity to comprehend what he taught, and ability to practice Kriya Yoga.

In recent years it has been said that one of Paramahansa Yogananda's missions was to restore the "original Christianity of Jesus and the original yoga of Krishna"—a perhaps noble endeavor that is impossible to accomplish. Historical records of the life of Jesus and of Krishna are few, and most of what has been written about them is conjecture—inference based on incomplete or inconclusive evidence. Christianity evolved after the death of Jesus. The historical Krishna is not known to have been a teacher of yoga. The Krishna portrayed in the Bhagavad Gita as a personification of supreme Consciousness is a fictional character created by the author for the purpose of describing yogic principles and practices.

How did Paramahansaji relate to people whose understanding of spiritual matters was limited or who were inclined to prefer fantasy to truth?

With disciples who were very close to him, he was forthright with his comments and guidance. With students who were not yet able to understand what he taught, he was patient and considerate.

While I was at the Phoenix center, Herbert Freed and I were invited by an SRF member to have dinner with her and her husband at their house a few miles from the city. While we were there, she showed us her art studio where she painted landscapes and portraits for her personal enjoyment. Before a large portrait of what appeared to be a likeness of a wise, ancient sage that she had painted, she said, "That is my master. He comes to me in dreams and visions and instructs me." I did not inquire about the portrait or her dreams and visions.

On the return drive to Phoenix, Herbert told me that my silence had been appropriate, and related the following anecdote:

"When she showed me that portrait last year and told me what she told you today, I was tempted to challenge her story. When I asked Master about it, he said, 'It's her fantasy. Don't tell her that. If you do, you will drive her away. In time, she will outgrow it.' "

Was Paramahansa Yogananda a strict vegetarian?

He preferred vegetarian foods and advised others to adopt a vegetarian diet, which he said was healthier and compatible with the ideal of harmlessness.

In the 1920s, in an endeavor to encourage his students to choose vegetarian foods, he experimented with gluten and created meat-substitute recipes. I once heard him say, in a joking manner, "I can make mock liver and onions, and chicken, that you will think is the real thing."

I was told by a few disciples that if he was a dinner guest at the home of a person who did not know that he preferred vegetarian foods, if meat was served he might taste it and make a courteous, appropriate comment rather than make an issue of the matter.

Paramahansaji's mind-body constitution appeared to be a combination of kapha and pitta as described in ayurvedic literature. His upper body was thick; his hips and legs were thin. He was patient, could endure long hours of physical activity, and could fast from foods without discomfort, which are kapha characteristics. His pitta characteristics were evident by his keen powers of perception and intelligence, purposefulness, persistence, energy, and creativity.

At times, he had to be attentive to his diet and exercise routines to maintain his ideal body weight. If he ate too much, he quickly gained weight. In India, in the 1930s, his friends insisted on preparing banquets in his honor. He gained sixty pounds, which he discarded when he returned to America.

During a visit to his desert retreat, I was having a light lunch with three brother disciples on the patio near Master's house. Master came out to chat with us. Seeing a soy-based cutlet on a plate on the table, he took a small piece of it, tasted it, and spat the solid bits onto the ground, near a hedge. With a mischievous smile and a twinkle in his eyes, he said, "If they (his disciple-secretaries) ask you if I ate anything out here, you tell them I didn't. You saw that I didn't eat it."

How many initiations are given in this Kriya Yoga tradition?

The first initiation, when kriya pranayama is taught and the initiate makes a firm commitment to discipleship, is the most important one. When proficiency in meditation practice has been acquired, supplemental meditation techniques may be taught with or without a formal initiation ceremony.

Lahiri Mahasaya taught kriya meditation techniques to his disciples in stages, giving further instructions as the disciple's capacity to practice increased. Paramahansaji also did this. Some Kriya Yoga gurus give four initiations, others give more, as determined by how they choose to teach. There is no strict rule regarding the matter; a knowledgeable guru will teach in accord with the disciple's ability to learn and to practice.

The new initiate is told not to talk to others about what was taught when they were initiated because it is for them to know and practice; talking about it distracts attention from their practice and weakens the psychic bond between them and their guru. What is learned should be internalized.

The meditation methods which are taught by gurus in this Kriya Yoga tradition are not secrets; they have been described in several published works and are taught because they are effective when rightly used.

Some Kriya Yoga practitioners who have not yet diligently used the basic meditation techniques, or whose lives are not yet well-ordered, erroneously think that if they could learn advanced methods their spiritual progress would be more satisfying. Instead of effectively using what they know, they go from teacher to teacher, talk excessively with their friends about meditation practices, read a variety of books, or peruse Internet web sites in an endeavor to acquire the information they desire to have. They become confused and neglect their spiritual practices.

Paramahansaji said that samadhi could be experienced by using only a meditation mantra if one persisted until the mind was calm and awareness was clear. During a private talk with some disciples he advised one of them, whose concentration was easily distracted when using a mantra, to imagine that he was breathing through the spiritual eye. Doing that enabled him to more fully involve his attention with the process.

It is said that kriya pranayama practice refines the nervous system and causes changes in the brain that enable one to more easily experience clear states of consciousness. Does this mean that doing many kriya pranayamas is more useful than doing only a few of them?

Paramahansaji often said that concentrated practice of a few kriya pranayamas is more beneficial than doing many of them superficially. New meditators are usually advised to do twelve repetitions (once or twice a day), and to sit silently for a while in the tranquil state of consciousness that results from practice. "If you don't sit in the silence after practicing kriya [pranayama]," my guru said, "You would be like a person who prepared a delicious meal but doesn't partake of any of it."

After a few months of regular kriya pranayama practice, more repetitions can be done. Practice should be concentrated but not forceful. It is a mistake to presume that by doing an excessive number of repetitions one's spiritual evolution will be more rapid. Other factors, such as ethical behavior, a wholesome lifestyle, and sustained aspiration to be spiritually enlightened are equally important.

Did your guru recommend Hatha Yoga practice?

It was recommended, but not emphasized. If he could see the extent to which yoga has been accepted in our society today, he would be pleased. If he could see the many different ways in which Hatha Yoga is now promoted and taught, he would be mildly amused.

Bishnu Ghosh, a younger brother of Paramahansaji, was a well-known physical culturist in India. In 1939, when he was in southern California, he offered to teach Mr. Lynn advanced Hatha Yoga practices. When Mr. Lynn asked Master if he should learn and practice them, he was told, "If you do, you may lose your bliss." To another person, Master might have responded differently. At that time, because Mr. Lynn's Hatha Yoga routine was already satisfactory, he was advised to concentrate on perfecting his meditation practices.

Some people say that exceptional powers of perception and extraordinary functional abilities that one might have as a result of spiritual awakening should not be used to fulfill one's personal desires. Is this true?

What is recommended is that they not be used to satisfy egocentric inclinations. Acquired knowledge and skills should be wisely used to enhance our lives and the lives of others and to nurture and complete our spiritual awakening.

Is celibacy necessary for a person on the spiritual path?

Celibacy—being unmarried, especially if one has taken religious vows, or complete abstinence from sexual intercourse—is not necessary for a person on the spiritual path. A wholesome, compatible, romantic relationship can enhance one's physical, emotional, and spiritual well-being. Personal relationships that are not harmonious or meaningful should be avoided; they waste one's time, energies, and personal resources, and may contribute to mental and emotional unrest.

Members of some religious orders choose a lifestyle that allows them to focus their thoughts and energies on spiritual practices or to render service to others. Some people who are not members of a religious order, who are not married, choose to avoid relationships and activities which are not meaningful and circumstances which may complicate their lives or distract them from their major purposes. A person who chooses, and is comfortable with, a celibate lifestyle should not have feelings of pride or self-righteousness regarding their choice.

What is the most helpful way to use affirmations?

To affirm is to declare something to actually exist. To have the mental outlook, state of consciousness, or circumstances that you consider to be ideal for you, affirm what you want to experience. Choose an affirmation that defines the end result.

Example:

I am physically healthy, mentally alert, emotionally stable, spiritually aware, and in my right place in the universe. Everything in my life is now in divine order. I am peaceful, happy, and thankful.

Speak the affirmation aloud with conviction a few times. Speak it quietly a few times. Whisper it a few times. Mentally affirm it a few times. Internalize it. Feel and know it to be true. Rest in the silence for a few moments. Maintain your awareness of what you affirmed at all times. If you can do something to actualize what you affirmed, do it.

What is the best way to learn how to practice Kriya Yoga?

The best way to learn anything of value is to find a reliable source of information. Read Patanjali's yoga-sutras. It is also helpful to learn from someone who is knowledgeable.

I would like to have a spiritual teacher (guru) to instruct and guide me. How can I find the right teacher for me?

Don't try to find one. Prepare yourself by acquiring useful knowledge from reliable sources and applying it in your daily life. When reading books or obtaining information from other sources, use your discrimination to determine what is true and worthwhile. Live wholesomely and constructively. Cultivate optimism. Meditate daily. Aspire to be fully awake. Improve your intellectual and intuitive powers. Pray for guidance and be receptive to your highest good. If you are destined to have a teacher who can instruct and guide you, supportive events and circumstances will unfold to make it possible.

Is it difficult to be Self-realized and spiritually enlightened?

It can be difficult when one is identified with ordinary states of consciousness. It can be easy when one sincerely aspires to be Self-realized and spiritually enlightened (knowledgeable) and does what is necessary to purify their mind and clarify their consciousness. Self-realization is a matter of personal choice.

You have said that a Kriya Yoga initiate who did not have a per-sonal relationship with Paramahansa Yogananda should not con-sider themselves to be his disciple. Is there a possibility that a guru-disciple relationship was established in a previous incar-nation? If that relationship has not been established and one feels a strong attunement with Paramahansaji, what should one do?

Many individuals who think that Paramahansa Yogananda is their guru because they are attracted to him, are inspired by his writings, or were initiated into Kriya Yoga practices by some-one, have been misinformed, are emotionally immature, or prefer fantasy to truth. While reading his books or hearing a recording of one of his talks can be helpful, it not possible for them to be personally taught and guided by him.

If a relationship with Paramahansaji was established in a previous incarnation, and one knows this with certainty, when or if guidance is necessary, it can be obtained from one of his successors or from another qualified Kriya Yoga teacher.

I would like to know more about the stages of Self- and God-Real-ization that can result in liberation of consciousness.

The four states of consciousness to know are: 1) the waking state; 2) the dream state; 3) unconsciousness, as when dream-less sleep occurs; 4) superconsciousness, of which there can be several stages. Self-realization is different from ordinary states of consciousness. During superconsciousness, our awareness may be partially or fully identified with an object of attention or be unsupported and devoid of modifying characteristics (thoughts, emotions, or other influences).

The four stages of refined superconsciousness are:

1. Superconscious states in relationship to memories and mental concepts, during which one may be inclined to compare the experience with prior states of consciousness or with what others have said about superconscious states.

2. Superconscious states without memories or ideas. Attention and awareness is so fully absorbed in an object of contemplation that all sense of "otherness" is absent.

3. Examination of subtle essences or aspects of the object contemplated. One may be inclined to inquire into subtle aspects of the mind, intellect, ego, or supreme Consciousness and its processes of cosmic manifestation. A sense of "I am looking at this" prevails.

4. Spontaneously revealed knowledge of subtle essences or aspects formerly examined. At this stage, pure consciousness along with knowledge is "self-shining."

Beyond these stages is existence-being-realization without the support of an object of attention. When Self-realization is complete, it permanently persists whether one is meditating or is engaged in normal activities. The final stage is constant Self- and God-realization which results in complete liberation of consciousness. Erroneous ideas and illusions are absent.

I want to be able to meditate effectively. How can I do it?

Decide to meditate every day. Choose a suitable time and place. When possible, meditate at the same time every day. If you are a novice, meditate for fifteen to twenty minutes. You can meditate longer when you become more proficient.

• Sit upright in a comfortable chair. If you prefer to sit in a cross-legged posture, sit like that.
• Put your attention and awareness in the front and upper region of the brain.
• If you like to pray, pray to invoke an awareness of God. If you are an initiate, mentally acknowledge your guru and the lineage of gurus.
• If meditation flows spontaneously, let it flow.
• If meditation does not flow spontaneously, you may use a medi-

tation technique to calm your mind, clarify your awareness, and improve your concentration. A mantra may be helpful. Any word or word-phrase that appeals to you can be used. To use the word "peace," "Om," or "God," speak the word mentally. Example: "Om, Om, Om, Om" in a steady stream for as long as necessary. If thoughts interrupt your concentration or your attention wanders, resume the use of the mantra. Continue until your attention is focused, then let the mantra fade away.

If you use a word-phrase, mentally speak the first word as you breath in; mentally speak the second word when you exhale. An example of a word-phrase is "Om-God." Sanskrit mantras that can be used in this way are *hong-sau* (saw) and *so-ham* (hum). If you are an initiate, practice the techniques as they were taught to you.

• Sit in the peaceful, thought-free silence for a while.
• To conclude, open your eyes. Retain your peacefulness as you turn your attention to your duties.

This easy routine is suitable for anyone. Regular practice will reduce stress, strengthen the immune system, slow biologic aging processes, improve powers of concentration, enable one to think more rationally, and nurture spiritual growth.

Advanced practice of meditation:

Proceed as above until your attention is internalized, but sit longer in the silence with attention and awareness focused in the crown chakra. If you hear a sound-frequency, let your attention and awareness be attracted to it. Contemplate your pure-conscious essence of being. Relax. Let your innate urge to have your consciousness restored to wholeness determine the outcome of your practice session.

Avoid anxiety about the results of practice. Meditate on a regular schedule and skillfully live your life. Avoid talking about your meditative experiences with others. Concentrate on unfolding and actualizing your innate, divine potential.

How is Meditation on Om Practiced?

Om (also AUM) is described as having four parts: *a*, *u*, *m*, and a dot used to indicate a nasal humming sound when it is chanted. These are related to four states of consciousness: waking, dreaming sleep, deep sleep, and the Self-knowing, transcendental state.

Audible and mental chanting of Om is useful. Listening to it while meditating is more useful. The progressive stages of practice can be:

• With attention and awareness focused in the spiritual eye and crown chakra, listen in the ears (or space around your head) to hear subtle sounds behind the ringing sounds that may first be heard. Continue to listen until the sound that is heard is constant. Consider that sound to be an aspect of the Om vibration.
• Merge your attention and awareness in the sound until you are aware of being one with it. Meditate *in* Om.
• With awareness in the crown chakra, direct attention to the source from which Om emanates until you are established in pure Consciousness.

When meditating in Om, remain alert, yet surrendered. Avoid impatient, effort-driven concentration. Sit until your mind is calm and meditation flows spontaneously.

Meditating in Om can result in comprehension of what it is, its characteristics, and its source. That is why meditation in Om is said to be the direct way to Self- and God-knowledge.

If preliminary meditation techniques are used (recitation of or listening to a mantra, pranayama, or concentration on a chosen form or aspect of ultimate Reality), the final practice is to have attention and awareness in the crown chakra.

When meditating in Om, transitory, subjective perceptions of visions or sounds (other than Om) should be ignored. When the mind is calm, only absolute silence and awareness of pure being will prevail.

To have wholesome desires and intentions easily fulfilled, Paramahansa Yogananda advised his disciples to merge their awareness in Om and "float" their desires and intentions in it. When doing this, avoid willfulness, and inclinations to attempt to force anything to happen. While one with Om, release your desires and intentions into it and it will provide the support and good fortune that you need and deserve.

After meditating in Om, when conviction that your desires and intentions for your total well-being and spiritual growth will be fulfilled is established, supportive events will spontaneously occur to make possible their fulfillment.

When your awareness is merged in Om, a mere impulse of desire or intention is sufficient to cause predictable effects. Working at this level of awareness and understanding is more subtle, and more reliable, than attempting to pray for results or using affirmations. When praying for results, you may have difficulty believing that your prayers will be effective. When using an affirmation, you may have difficulty assuming and maintaining a conviction that what you affirm is real. When you are established in Self-knowledge and identified with Om, you are where objective phenomena originate, and are conscious of the wholeness of which all relative events and things are parts or aspects.

It may be that creative ideas arise in your mind or that you are impelled to perform useful actions. Act on your creative ideas and perform useful actions when you can. When you do not know what to do to help yourself, stay anchored in Self-knowledge and the Om vibration. Welcome the good fortune that is freely provided for you.

Why is it recommended that Kriya Yoga meditation practices not be mixed with other practices? Please provide examples.

One can, of course, observe traditional religious practices: Christian, Jewish, Hindu, Buddhist, or others. It is not useful to mix kriya meditation practices with those of traditions or systems which do not have the same ideals or purposes. Most "new age" practices (hypnosis, channeling, preoccupation with auras, or so-called "quick enlightenment" methods) should be avoided, as well as any other practices which may distract one from useful spiritual endeavors or cause mental confusion.

Explain more about the avatar concept. What does it mean to be an avatar? Are there any avatars presently on our planet?

An *avatar* is generally thought of as an unrestricted manifestation of God in human form. I do not know of any such incarnations. An objective examination of the lives of individuals, past and present, who have been referred to as avatars reveals that they experienced a variety of personal challenges before awakening to Self-realization. If the fullness of God actually incarnated, the event would be so dramatic that there would be no doubt about the matter.

It is common for devotees of a saintly person to refer to that person as an avatar because they 1) believe it; 2) want to believe it; 3) think that person had (or has) qualities or abilities that are exceptional in comparison to people whose awareness and abilities are ordinary.

One has only to visit a place where a presumed avatar resides to see that conditions there are not always harmonious and that the devotees who are there are not always healthy-minded, rational, or spiritually conscious. If God were actually present in a body with unrestricted knowledge and power, everything and everyone in relationship to that manifestation of God would be immediately transformed and more people in our present era would be spiritually enlightened.

Some disciples of Paramahansa Yogananda are emphatic in their belief that he was an avatar and seem to derive a degree of comfort from their belief. Master viewed himself and all souls as waves on the ocean of infinite life, preferring to acknowledge the whole rather than its aspects. When he was asked by a disciple if he had been known as a certain widely admired saint in a previous incarnation, he said, "What does it matter what names are given to the waves that rise and fall on the surface of the ocean?"

It has been rumored that one of Master's former incarnations was that of Arjuna. This cannot be true because Arjuna is a fictional name used by the author of the Bhagavad Gita to represent self-control and resolute will to accomplish noble purposes, helpful characteristics for a spiritual aspirant that are related to the lumbar chakra.

Is it necessary to experience a "breathless state" to experience samadhi?

It is not necessary for breathing to cease. When breathing is slow and shallow, mental states are usually calm, awareness may be more clear, and superconsciousness may more easily be elicited. There are gaps between thoughts that occur in the mind and changes that occur in awareness. Look for those empty spaces and become familiar with what it is like when thoughts and changes in awareness no longer distract your attention or modify your awareness. With practice, you will be able to assume a thought-free state of clear awareness at will. If thoughts are present when you meditate, you can learn to disregard them. When engaged in ordinary activities, you can be Self-aware while thinking and acting.

When asked to describe "Kriya Yoga," what should I say?

Define the words. Explain that a *kriya* is an "action." *Yoga* is the bringing together of attention and awareness with something or with one's essence of being. *Kriya Yoga practices* include mental, moral, and physical discipline as may be required; study of higher realities; and purification of ego consciousness in order to be Self- and God-aware. This way of life can be viewed as a natural way to facilitate spiritual growth. It is for everyone, everywhere, regardless of their personal history or cultural circumstances.

Some people say the physical world is real. Others say it is an illusion. Is it real, or not real?

Because physical things can be observed, examined, and measured, they exist. When philosophers say that the universe is not real, they mean that it does not exist apart from the cosmic forces which produced and sustain it and is not as it superficially appears to be. The one Consciousness which emanated the universe is the only self-existent Reality. Matter is composed of atoms and their fine parts and forces.

The universe is not an illusion. When we do not accurately comprehend it, our mistaken perception may result in our own faulty beliefs or opinions.

If the universe had a beginning and will eventually cease to exist, what is the purpose of our being here?

Spiritually enlightened people declare that the universe provides a variety of opportunities for life to express and for souls to actualize their innate potential. Some materialistic people who do not apprehend higher realties say that human beings are accidents of evolution. When we know that we are spiritual beings and know that the universe exists because of interactions of cosmic forces, we can also know that when a physical universe dissolves (after trillions of solar years), its component aspects (space, time, and cosmic forces) will still exist in the field of primordial Nature from which it was first emanated. After a duration of nonmanifestation, another universe is produced and life is eventually able to emerge in it. The manifestation, evolution, and dissolution of universes are periodic events.

I sometimes wonder if I will ever be spiritually enlightened.

Your comment reminds me of a disciple who was devotional, but could not (or would not) control his personal behaviors.

When someone asked Paramahansaji about him, he said, "I prayed to know his future and was told that he would be liberated in this incarnation."

The person who had inquired, said, "I don't know how that can be possible."

Paramahansaji chuckled, then replied, "I don't either, but that is what I was told, so it must be true."

You will certainly be spiritually enlightened because it is your destiny to be fully awake. At the core of your being, you are already whole and knowledgeable.

I am reluctant to make a commitment to discipleship because I am afraid of what might be required of me and what changes might occur in my life.

What will be required, by self-decided choice, is your total dedication to the spiritual path. The changes that occur in you and in your circumstances will be beneficial. You will have to decide. Do you want to be as you are? Or do you sincerely want to actualize your full potential as a spiritual being?

Have you known any individuals who were (or are) fully Self- and God-realized as a result of their practice of Kriya Yoga?

I know of only a few whom Paramahansaji said were Self- and God-realized, or would be, in their present incarnation. I cannot determine a person's degree of Self-realization unless I have an opportunity to closely observe them. I do know that many devotees have made the mistake of being satisfied with having a sense of God-communion rather than aspiring to be fully spiritually enlightened. Some of them were complacent because they wanted to be receptive to "God's will" for them. One who believes that Self-realization is solely determined by God will be inclined to hope and wait rather than do what is necessary to purify the mind, refine the body, and clarify their awareness. Some devotees who feel that their role is to be a servant of God are influenced by sentiment and not by reason or an innate urge to be fully awake. They mistakenly think that they cannot be fully awake or are reluctant to assume a radical adjustment of viewpoint that would allow them to be Self- and God-realized.

Some people are attracted to a spiritual path because they desire better health, peace of mind, or material success. Some read metaphysical literature and passively pray or meditate to avoid the challenge of responsible living. Some associate with friends who share their interest in spirituality because they enjoy social interaction. Only a few among the many I have known who were attracted to the Kriya Yoga path were sincere in their desire to be Self- and God-realized and willing to persist in the right way until their aspiration was fulfilled.

Most of the more than one hundred thousand individuals who were initiated by Paramahansaji during his thirty-one years in America did not maintain a relationship with him or continue with their studies and meditation practices. Of the more than ten thousand individuals who were initiated by me during the past fifty years, perhaps ten percent of them have maintained contact with me and not all of them practice intensively.

What others do, or don't do, should not overly concern us. Our resolve to be spiritually awake should be decisive.

I want to meditate, and I have tried to do it. It is difficult for me to sit still and to control my thoughts.

Learn how to meditate, and practice on a regular schedule. Before long, it will be easy to sit quietly and thoughts will be easily ignored. Avoid trying so hard to succeed. Relax, and let meditation flow naturally. If thoughts persist, think about the fact that you are a spiritual being and about your relationship with the Infinite.

Some people have difficulty when they sit to meditate (or start to do anything that is worthwhile) because they think, or talk, too much instead of entering into the process and letting the desired results naturally occur.

With so much unrest in the world today, what is the best way to relate to events without becoming overwhelmed by them?

Train yourself to always be established in Self-knowing and view transitory events with an objective mental attitude while attending to your duties and responsibilities. Live in this changing world without being emotionally reactive to what you observe and you will be a positive influence.

Global unrest and conflict are symptoms of confusion and frustration that so many people are experiencing. Some of it is due to ignorance and selfishness. The only permanent cure for the many problems which are now widely reported is for caring, capable people to replace them with solutions which are realistic and compassionate.

What is the most useful way to pray for the welfare of others?

Pray verbally, mentally, or simply and sincerely wish for their highest good. If someone asks you to pray for them, see beyond their problem or need to what can be most ideal for them and believe that to be true.

Beyond the stage of verbal, mental, or wishing prayer is spiritual help offered impersonally. For this, be still until you are consciously established in awareness of God's wholeness, then mentally acknowledge the people with whom you want to share your God-awareness. There is no need to try to send healing or blessing influence to them. Mentally and spiritually "invite" them to merge their awareness with your awareness of God, then let the results be in accord with their receptivity. In this way, you are not trying to do anything for them or attempting to cause a specific effect or outcome.

When your Self- and God-consciousness is constant, when someone thinks about or talks to you, even if you are not aware of their needs, you will be a point of contact for them to receive a flow of grace from the Source.

I was recently initiated into Kriya Yoga meditation practices. What else should I do?

When you were initiated, you were given general lifestyle guidelines and specific instruction in the practice of meditation techniques. Initiation should be viewed as an occasion during which ordinary, nonuseful mental attitudes and behaviors are renounced and constructive mental attitudes and behaviors are chosen. Live a balanced, uncomplicated life. Cultivate the virtues. Improve your understanding of your true nature and your relationship with the Infinite. Meditate daily to the stage of superconsciousness. Do what is important to do. Fervently aspire to be Self-realized and liberated. Persist in your right endeavors. Avoid useless metaphysical speculation. Cultivate Self-knowing and endeavor to be in that Self-knowing state of consciousness at all times.

Why do some Kriya Yoga practitioners who seem peaceful and devotional still have erroneous beliefs?

They don't use their intellectual powers to discern what is

true or they may not be well-informed. Some of them are confused because of trying to adapt philosophical concepts on which authentic spiritual enlightenment practices are based, to false traditional religious beliefs acquired when they were children or young adults. They also habitually associate with friends who think as they do.

When they meditate, they are inclined to be satisfied with having only a sense of peace or blissfulness which they mistakenly presume to be evidence of communion with God. If they regularly experienced higher samadhi states and used their powers of discernment, and common sense, their knowledge of the facts of life would be flawless.

What are the stages of Self-realization mentioned in this quote from Patanjali's yoga-sutras?

For the yogi, the elimination of obstacles to Self-realization may be experienced in seven successive stages. (2:27)

During the *first stage*, one becomes aware of subliminal influences that need to be resisted, weakened, and eliminated; the erroneous ideas that need to be discarded; and the faulty behaviors to avoid to allow further spiritual growth to occur.

At the *second stage*, subconscious influences that have the potential to cause pain or misfortune are resisted, weakened, and neutralized.

At the *third stage*, refined states of consciousness can easily be discerned and examined.

At the *fourth stage*, one's relationship to the mind and to internal and external conditions is clearly comprehended.

At the *fifth stage*, subliminal influences no longer cause changes to occur in one's mind and awareness. Self-realization spontaneously occurs.

At the *sixth stage*, God-realization, experience along with knowledge of the reality of God, occurs.

At the *seventh stage* the mind is illumined and one's consciousness is liberated.

I enjoy praying to saints and the gurus of our tradition who are no longer in this world. Now and then, I wonder if the satisfying results that I sometimes experience are because of their response or are the results of my own prayers and personal expectations.

When you pray to a saint, your concept of that person is a point of contact with a larger reality. The beneficial response is due to either your own expectation or flows of grace from the Source.

What can I do to become more cosmic conscious?

Clarify and expand your consciousness. Aspire to perceive all that can be perceived and to know all that is useful for you to know. As your capacity to perceive and to know increases, cosmic conscious states will be experienced. A person who is thirsty may want to drink a large quantity of water, but the amount of water that one can drink is determined by the size of one's stomach. Your aspiration to be cosmic conscious will be actualized in accord with your capacity to be aware of the wholeness of life.

When you meditate, expand your consciousness. Imagine that you are omnipresent. At other times, remember that you abide in the ocean of Consciousness and that everything in the universe exists in that Consciousness. It can also be helpful to be aware at the crown chakra and to feel that you are not confined to your mind or body.

I am trying to acquire an understanding of God. Is it necessary to have an intellectual understanding of God before having direct experience of God?

An intellectual understanding of God will enable you to think more rationally about your relationship with God, live more effectively, and better comprehend what you experience and perceive when direct experience of God occurs.

It is not possible to intellectually know everything about God because intellectual powers are limited even when they are highly developed. When your intuitive powers, which are superior to intellectual powers, are highly developed, you will be able to more easily comprehend the reality of God.

If it is important that we know the reality of God, why don't more people have this knowledge?

Having one's awareness identified with a mistaken sense of self is the primary obstacle to knowing the reality of God. One is then inclined to think of the body and/or personality as their real identity. A person whose awareness is confined by ego-sense is inclined to think that they might have a spiritual essence or soul and that if God exists, God is apart from them and unknowable.

Some other obstacles to God-knowing are:

• Lack of interest in knowing God.
• Interest in knowing God is superficial.
• Mental confusion, emotional unrest, preoccupation with mundane interests and concerns, or intellectual laziness.
• Intellectual and intuitive powers may be weak or psychological problems may interfere with rational thinking.
• The nervous system may not yet be sufficiently developed or refined to accommodate higher states of consciousness.
• Even if a person is healthy and mentally competent, egotism (an inflated sense of self-importance) may interfere with learning and comprehension.
• Complacent acceptance of erroneous ideas about God that comfort the mind or provide emotional satisfaction.

I have done my best to live a good life, yet my understanding of God has not improved very much. Doesn't living a good life have any value in relationship to spiritual growth?

If living an honest, moral, wholesome, helpful life resulted in God-knowledge, millions of people would now be spiritually enlightened. Right living can contribute to orderly personal relationships and psychological health, and provide a foundation for spiritual growth. Continue to live a good life and attend to your spiritual practices while improving your understanding of God and your role in the universe.

I feel good about my spiritual progress and how my life is improving. At times, however, memories of painful childhood experiences dominate my mind and cause feelings of shame and fear. How can I come to terms with these memories and no longer be troubled by them?

Although past events cannot be changed, you can learn to view memories without having mental or emotional reactions. When memories of unpleasant events elicit painful thoughts and feelings, do something that elicits feelings of pleasure. Take a brisk walk, do some physical exercises, or involve your attention with a worthwhile project. You may also replace unwanted thoughts and emotions with positive thoughts and emotional peace by breathing deeply a few times.

Use your will power to choose your thoughts and feelings. Remember that you are a spiritual being, superior to mental and emotional states.

What is the most effective way to awaken to higher stages of spiritual awareness?

Replace restrictive mental attitudes, emotions, behaviors, and (when possible) environmental conditions with attitudes, emotions, behaviors, and environmental conditions which are supportive of your aspirations. Satisfying spiritual growth will occur with your willing cooperation.

Expand your consciousness. Imagine what is possible for you to experience and believe with all your heart (being) that you can and will experience rapid spiritual awakening.

Avoid (when possible) intimate interactions with others who are complacently satisfied with a materialistic lifestyle.

Identify with intelligent, emotionally mature, spiritually aware people. Emulate their positive mental attitudes, clear states of consciousness, and useful behaviors.

Choose to be the person you want to be. Think thoughts you want to think. Do what you know you should do, and you will surely have the life-enhancing experiences and clear perceptions of higher realities you want to have. —

Unwaveringly aspire to be Self- and God-realized. Persist in the right way. Do everything you know to do to allow the natural processes of spiritual growth to occur. Have absolute faith in the outcome. See the end result in your mind's eye. Feel it in the core of your being. Cultivate serene joyfulness. Be happy. Be thankful that you are on the right course in life.

When friends ask why God allows pain and suffering in the world, what can I tell them?

To your friends who have a rigid, fundamentalist concept of God, there is not anything to be said that will be helpful. To your friends who are receptive to understanding, explain that God is not a cosmic person who causes pain or suffering. People cause their own misfortune by their thoughts and actions; are influenced by their environmental conditions or habitual personal relationships; have inherited tendencies that they may need to overcome; may be affected by changing social or economic conditions; or may be affected by the forces of Nature if they happen to be where the effects of earthquakes, severe storms, or other destructive natural events occur. The more spiritually conscious people are, the more likely it is that they will experience good fortune. Even during episodes of occasional misfortune, a person who is spiritually aware will be able to maintain their peace of mind.

I think that I am on the right spiritual path for me. Some of my friends are inclined to advise me to do some of the things they do that seem to me not to be useful. What should I do?

If you know that your path is right for you, avoid talking to others about your ideals and spiritual practices.

Can we make fast progress on the spiritual path if other people in the world are not as interested in spiritual matters as we are? What about the influence of the collective consciousness of the world's population? Does this affect us?

You can only be affected by external conditions by allowing yourself to be influenced. People whose awareness is ordinary usually experience what most people experience because they have similar states of consciousness, beliefs, and habits. One who engages in intensive spiritual practices and who has chosen a different, more beneficial way to think and live, attracts ideal, supportive circumstances and cooperates with evolutionary forces that assist their spiritual growth.

The more spiritually aware we are, the more influential are the enlivening and redemptive influences referred to as God's grace. Grace is available to everyone; it is increasingly expressive in our lives when we are receptive to it.

I am in the autumn of my earth life. Can I awaken to Self-and God-realization before I make my transition?

Aspire to be Self- and God-realized. Avoid preoccupation with thinking that time is a factor regarding spiritual growth. Train yourself to be alert. A sudden, revelatory adjustment of viewpoint can occur at any moment. Pray to be Self- and God-realized. Remain calm and peaceful.

Endeavor to have a long, healthy life that will allow you to accomplish all of your important purposes and awaken to higher stages of spiritual awareness. Remain devoted to your aspiration to be Self- and God-realized.

After Paramahansa Yogananda's transition in 1952, did you have any other spiritual teachers?

What I learned from my guru, and his transmission to me of his love, spiritual energy, and enlightened consciousness, has sustained me. Through the years, I have had many enjoyable spiritual friendships with other teachers: Ernest Holmes, Ernest Wilson, Neville Goddard, Manly Palmer Hall, Walter Lanyon, Masaharu Taniguchi, Joel Goldsmith (who informed me that he had practiced Kriya Yoga meditation methods that were taught to him by Paramahansaji), Swami Muktananda, Swami Rama, and others.

Besides right living, metaphysical study, and meditation practice, what else can be done to nurture spiritual awakening?

Until you are Self- and God-realized, constantly yearn to be fully awake. The emergence of your innate knowledge of your true nature and the reality of God can suddenly occur at any moment. To a person who asked Paramahansaji how one could know when Self- and God-knowledge was authentic, he replied, "You will know when you know."

Some yoga teachers say that one's ego must be eliminated. Is this true?

A sense of self as being distinct from the world and from other selves is necessary to enable us to relate to the world and to others. Egocentricity, being confined by a small sense of self, can and should be transcended because it is the primary obstacle to being Self-realized. When the ego is purified (not eliminated), we can view the world and all of our relationships with objectivity while being soul-centered. Our sense of self as being distinct from the world and from others is transcended when attention is internalized during our interludes of meditative superconsciousness (samadhi).

Did Paramahansa Yogananda recommend the establishment of spiritual communities?

In the last chapter ("At Encinitas in California") of the first edition of *Autobiography of a Yogi*, he described a conversation with a disciple, in 1945, during which he had said: "A project I have long considered is beginning to take definite form ... In these beautiful surroundings I have started a miniature world colony. A small harmonious group here may inspire other ideal communities over the earth. We shall arrange here many conferences ... inviting delegates from all lands. Flags of all nations will hang in our halls. As soon as possible I intend to start a Yoga Institute here."

While it was characteristic of my guru to want his plans to be immediately implemented and soon completed, he knew that some of them were premature. Of the latter kind, he said that he had sown the seeds [of specific projects] in the ethers that would produce ideal results in the course of time.

What was Paramahansa Yogananda's advice regarding how to overcome or eliminate troublesome karmic influences?

Subconscious conditionings, thoughts, beliefs, mental attitudes, states of consciousness, emotions, desires, habits, and actions are causative (karmic) influences which may produce effects which are either harmful and debilitating, constructive

and life-enhancing, or neither debilitating or life-enhancing.
The way to overcome troublesome karmic influences is to cultivate orderly, constructive thinking, replace beliefs with accurate
knowledge, nurture optimism, maintain a clear state of consciousness, choose to be emotionally stable, desire only what is beneficial, adopt good habits, and perform actions that will produce
positive results. Daily practice of superconscious meditation and
Kriya Yoga meditation techniques will purify the mind and eliminate harmful subconscious influences.

In 1950, my guru said, "When you first came to me, God took
fifty percent of your karma. The guru takes twenty-five percent.
The remaining twenty-five percent, you have to work out by yourself." His mention of percentages was not meant to be specific.
When one chooses a clearly defined course of right action, many
troublesome events can be avoided and flows of grace can be more
freely expressive. The guru's guidance and transmission of spiritual energy, and a disciple's attunement with the guru's God-
consciousness, weakens and neutralizes much of a disciple's
karma. The disciple's responsibility is to live right, cultivate innate spiritual capacities, and awaken to liberation of consciousness as quickly as possible.

*What are some of the most important things that you learned from
your guru?*

To always fervently aspire to be fully awake in God and to
always think and live in ways that allow spiritual awakening to
quickly occur.

Paramahansa Yogananda, circa 1948

Paramahansa Yogananda, middle 1920s

In meditation on the beach at Encinitas, California

Conducting a memorial service for Mahatma Gandhi at the
Hollywood, California, Self-Realization Fellowship Temple
Photo, Los Angeles Times, 1947

Paramahansa Yogananda with his guru, Swami Sri Yukteswar
in India, circa 1935

6

Paramahansa Yogananda blessing James Lynn (Rajasi Janakananda)
Summer 1951

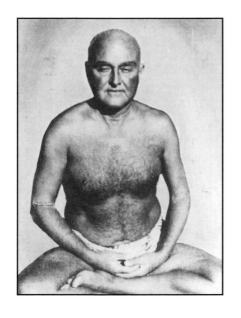

Top left: James Lynn

Top right: Oliver Black

Lower right: When I was the minister of the Self-Realization Fellowship Center in Phoenix, Arizona, 1952

Dedication of the SRF Lake Shrine (I am standing at the extreme right)

Paramahansa Yogananda one hour before his transition

Small attic room in Paramahansa Yogananda's Kolkata (Calcutta)
family home where he meditated during his early teenage years

Top: Center for Spiritual Awareness headquarters and retreat center, Lakemont, Georgia
Bottom: CSA members and friends during a week long summer meditation retreat, August 2000

Top: My lecture at the Ramana Maharishi Center,
Bangalore, India, January 2005
Bottom: Following one of my lectures in Bangalore,
India, October 2002

Top: During my second Japan visit in 1978
Bottom: Truth students at one of my lectures for Seicho-No-Ie
in Rio de Janeiro, Brazil

With CSA Ministers in Accra, Ghana (Samuel Sasu, in white garment standing beside me, is the director of CSA West Africa)

With European CSA members and friends, Munich, Germany, 2000

In the Meditation Hall at Center for Spiritual Awareness headquarters

APPENDIX

The Lineage of Gurus

A spiritually enlightened guru in the Himalayas, who is best known as Babaji, revived this Kriya Yoga tradition in the 19th century and chose a disciple, Lahiri Mahasaya, to make it available to truth seekers in all walks of life.

Babaji (father who is highly respected) is a common title used in India when referring to a virtuous or holy man. *Mataji* (mother who is respected) is the title used for a woman. The Babaji of this Kriya Yoga tradition is little known because he is usually secluded in the Himalayas with a few spiritually advanced disciples. He is believed to have been embodied for several hundred years.

My guru said that Babaji's mission of assisting people to spiritual fulfillment in our current era is not confined to this Kriya Yoga tradition. He has been known by various names at different times and places. Some titles of respect given him by disciples of Lahiri Mahasaya, and others, are Mahamuni Baba ("Great Silent Father"), Mahayogi ("Great Yogi"), and Shiva Baba (used to indicate the transformative influence).

Paramahansaji referred to Babaji as a mahavatar, a "great (maha) incarnation of divine qualities." There is some evidence to indicate that he was known to the village people in the Nainital District of the Himalayas in the last decade of the 19th century and the first two decades of the 20th century. Claims that have been recently made by several people, that Babaji personally or telepathically authorized them to teach or that he speaks through them, are false.

The Wisdom of Lahiri Mahasaya

One [supreme] Self is the ultimate Reality. It is the source of everything. The soul is immortal. God's attributes permeate it. Let your spiritual path be God-communion.

When the movements of awareness are transcended during meditation practice, consciousness is purified and oneness with the supreme Self is realized. Then the truth seeker's consciousness and supreme Consciousness are experienced as one.

Meditation is practice of conscious awareness of God within. It is the constant remembrance of the transcendental Spirit. God is revealed within us when our awareness is made pure by liberating it from all concepts of duality and finitude.

When the mind is serene, the reality of God is reflected in it. God, all-pervading and eternal, transcends the mind and the intellect.

Meditation results in divine revelation. From the reality of one's being arises perception and realization of the pure Self, the indwelling Divinity. Self-realization is conscious cognition of our absolute identity with God, the Self-revelation of our true nature by the illumination of pure consciousness.

The mind is the link between the soul and the senses. Divine perceptions are acquired when the senses are spiritualized. Joy, sweetness, and exultation fill the entire being when the senses are purified and inspired by the purity of the soul.

Each person is responsible for his or her inner life—which is the creation of one's thoughts, desires, feelings, and ideals.

Shyamacharan Lahiri (Mahasaya)
Disciple of Mahavatar Babaji
September 30, 1828 – September 26, 1895

In the village of Ghurni, Nadia district, in Bengal, on September 30, 1828, a soul who was to play an influential role in introducing Kriya Yoga to the multitudes was born into the Lahiri family and given the name Shyamacharan. In later years he would be known as Lahiri Mahasaya, one whose mind is large (*maha*) or expanded.

At school, Lahiri was exposed to English, Sanskrit, Urdu, Hindi, Bengali, and Persian languages. At eighteen years of age he was married to Kashimoni Devi and in the years that followed, five children were born, three sons and two daughters.

Lahiri Mahasaya was employed in Banaras (Varanasi) as a clerk in the British government military engineering department. Attentive to his work, family, and community duties, he also practiced meditation and read the Bhagavad Gita and other scriptures in the privacy of his home on Chowsatti Ghat Lane which leads to the Ganges River.

In 1861, he was temporarily transferred to Ranikhet, in the foothills of the Himalayas. While wandering in the hills on Drongiri Mountain because he had been told by the local people that "saints lived there," he encountered a young man who took him to a cave to meet Babaji.

With Babaji's blessings, Lahiri remembered a previous incarnation when they were together. Within two weeks he was taught a variety of meditation techniques and was formally initiated. The momentum of his previous spiritual practices enabled him to quickly become proficient in samadhi practice.

As Lahiri prepared to return to Banaras, he asked his newly-found guru for permission to initiate others who, like himself, had family and secular responsibilities. After a brief discussion, Babaji said, "Give kriya initiation to those who are honest and who will practice."

Lahiri initiated over five thousand devotees during his remaining years. He instructed them, "Don't tell anyone that I am your guru and don't tell them that you are practicing these methods." He wanted his disciples to follow his example: to live quietly, attend to their duties, and practice meditation privately. He advised most of his young male disciples to marry and told them that a well-balanced, secular life could provide a firm foundation for their spiritual practices.

He allowed his commentaries on twenty-six scriptures to be published by one of his disciples and made available to kriya initiates. No organized publicity endeavors on his behalf were permitted because he preferred to teach and initiate only those truth seekers who were sincere.

When Paramahansa Yogananda was one year old, his parents, who were disciples of Lahiri Mahasaya, took him to their guru's home to be blessed. Holding the child on his lap, he pronounced, "Your son will be a great spiritual engine and will carry many souls to God."

When Babaji met Sri Yukteswar in 1894, he told him to inform Lahiri that his present incarnation was soon to be concluded. Six months before his transition, Lahiri told his wife about his plans to leave his body during the month of September, 1895. On the 26th day of that month, which was the occasion for celebrating Mahastami, the second day of worship of a Divine Mother aspect of God as Durga (one of many aspects of God's creative energy), a ritual was being performed in the home of a neighbor. During this religious rite, the most significant moment is at the transition of the phase of the moon as it becomes brighter from the eighth to the ninth day. At that moment, Lahiri opened his eyes, closed them, and left his body. His body was cremated the next day.

Swami Sri Yukteswar (Priya Nath Karar)
Disciple of Lahiri Mahasaya
May 10, 1855 – March 9, 1936

Because of Sri Yukteswar's exceptional intellectual and intuitive powers, Paramahansa Yogananda referred to him as a Jnanavatar ("incarnation of knowledge"). Yukteswar (*yuk*, union, and *Ishwara*, the aspect of God that regulates cosmic processes) was the name given to him when he was ordained as a swami.

As a young adult, he attended college, but dropped out when he disagreed with one of his teachers. He privately studied anatomy, ayurveda, and Vedic astrology, and read the Bhagavad Gita and other scriptures. He was married, fathered a daughter, and provided for his family by managing family-owned properties. After his wife died at an early age, he sought spiritual advice from various teachers until he met Lahiri Mahasaya and was initiated by him. After he had practiced yogic disciplines for ten years, his guru gave him permission to initiate others.

At Babaji's request, he wrote a small book, *The Holy Science*, in which he explained the relationships between world events and cosmic time-cycles, described some of the compatible teachings of various religions, and shared his insights regarding the spiritual path. He also wrote a commentary on the Bhagavad Gita. He established two ashrams for the training of young, male disciples: in Puri, near the Bay of Bengal, and Serampore, near Calcutta. He also regularly visited many remote villages to teach Kriya Yoga practices and initiate disciples.

Sri Yukteswar departed from this world on March 9, 1936. His body was buried in the garden of his Puri ashram on the following day, during the last rites conducted by Paramahansa Yogananda. A small temple shrine was later constructed over his grave. A few weeks before Sri Yukteswar left his body, he instructed Paramahansaji to be responsible for managing his ashrams and provided information regarding the settling of his

The Wisdom of Swami Sri Yukteswar

Only a few individuals can [easily] rise above the influence of their professed creeds and find absolute harmonious accord in the truths propagated by all great faiths. People who are engrossed in mundane concerns need the help and guidance of those holy beings who bring light to humanity. All creatures, from the highest to the lowest, are eager to realize three things: existence, consciousness, and bliss.

God, the only Reality in the universe, is not comprehensible by the average person until awareness is elevated above the attributes of Nature.

When, by inference, the true nature of the universe and the relation between it and one's essence of being is known, and when one knows that lack of understanding causes souls to forget their true Self and experience suffering, one wishes to be relieved from misfortune. Freedom from the bondage of that ignorance then becomes the primary aim of life.

Moral courage, when it is firmly established, removes all obstacles to salvation [liberation of consciousness]: hatred, shame, fear, grief, condemnation of others, racial prejudice, pride of ancestry, and egotism.

When rested by kriya pranayama practice, the nervous system is refreshed. If one daily rests the nervous system in this way, the physical body is vitalized. Life and death come under the control of the yogi who perseveres in the practice of [this] pranayama.

By practicing kriya pranayama as advised by the guru, the sound of Om spontaneously manifests. Breathing becomes regulated and physical aging is slowed.

estate. "I leave everything in your hands," he said. "You will be able to successfully sail the boat of your life and that of the organization to the divine shores."

Paramahansa Yogananda (Mukunda Lal Ghosh)
Disciple of Swami Sri Yukteswar
January 5, 1893 – March 7, 1952

My guru was born at Gorakhpur, in northeastern India, where he lived until his family moved to Calcutta during his eleventh year. Of his parent's four sons and four daughters, he was the second son and fourth child. Both parents were disciples of Lahiri Mahasaya, whose picture was on the family altar in their home. His father was a railroad company executive and a director of a small bank which he had helped to organize. His mother died when he was eleven years of age.

When he was twelve years old, he meditated for two days in a small attic room in the family home. After the meditation session, as he was going down the stairs, he encountered one of his sisters whose arm had been injured. When he touched her, her healing was instantaneous. Years later in one of his lectures in America, he referred to that meditation experience as "My Forty-Eight Hours in Eternity."

Meditation practices were learned from his father and from his Sanskrit tutor, a disciple of Lahiri Mahasaya. He met Sri Yukteswar, in 1910, when he was seventeen, and began a ten-year period of intensive spiritual training. Soon after his graduation from college, in 1914, when he was initiated into the swami order by Sri Yukteswar, he chose Yogananda: God-union (*yog*) bliss (*ananda*) as his monastic name.

In 1917, he founded a residential school for boys, with classes for their secular education as well as yoga practice. While meditating at the school, in a vision he saw many people whom he intuitively knew would be his students and disciples in America.

When he was asked to speak at a conference of religious liberals in Boston, Massachusetts, he accepted the invitation. His father's generous financial assistance enabled him to travel by boat to Boston and to remain there after the conference. When his father gave him the money for his travel fare, he said, "I do not do this as your father, who wants you to say in India. I do this as a disciple of Lahiri Mahasaya."

When Master told his guru that he had been invited to speak at the conference in Boston, Sri Yukteswar said, "If you go now, all doors will open for you."

Before leaving India, when Master prayed for Babaji's blessing and guidance, Babaji came to him and assured him that Kriya Yoga would "ultimately spread to all lands."

Master conducted public lectures, spoke at churches and colleges, and taught classes in Boston and other New England communities for three years, and accepted his first American disciples. When he told his students about his plan to travel and teach more widely, they donated five thousand dollars to support the project. During the next few years, he lectured to large audiences in the major cities of the United States and initiated more than one hundred thousand people. He was welcomed by civic and business leaders in many cities. In Washington, D.C., his lectures attracted more than three thousand people and he was invited to visit President Calvin Coolidge in the White House.

Of the many people who attended lectures and classes, but did not fully comprehend what he taught or continue with their spiritual practices after he left their community, he said, "I was planting seeds in their subconscious which might later sprout and grow." Among those who came to his lectures and were initiated, several became lifelong disciples.

In 1925, during his first public lectures in Los Angeles, Master looked for a site where a permanent headquarters could be established. In the Highland Park section of Los Angeles, when he saw a ten-acre estate with a sixty-room hotel, on Mount Washington, he told his friends who were with him, "This place feels like ours!" When he discovered that the property was for sale, and informed his students about it, they donated twenty-five thousand dollars for the down payment. Some of his students were invited to live and work there with him.

During Master's 1935-36 India visit, Sri Yukteswar acknowledged him as a *paramahansa*: one who is able to flawlessly discern truth from untruth while living freely in the world. Enroute to India, he lectured in London to large audiences. In India, he spoke in several cities, visited ashrams and saints, and obtained more information about Lahiri Mahasaya's life that he included in his autobiography.

Returning to America, he concentrated on the training of disciples, regularly lectured and taught classes in California, wrote articles and books, and supervised the construction of new temples.

In the late 1940s, with "only a little more work to be done" to fulfill his mission, he went more frequently to his secluded retreat house in the desert, to meditate and to complete his writing projects.

To the end of his earth life, Paramahansa Yogananda lived as he advised others to live. A few months before his passing, while talking with a few of his disciples, he said, "Discard the false belief that there is a separation between spiritual and material life. Perform your duties skillfully. All work is purifying if it is done with the right motive. If you sometimes fail to accomplish your purpose, don't be discouraged. That is the best time to sow the seeds of success. In everything that you do, express your limitless soul qualities."

GLOSSARY

absolute Perfect, complete. Pure, not mixed. Not limited.

actualize To realize in action. Goals are actualized when they are accomplished. Abilities are actualized when they are expressed.

affirm Latin *affirmare*, to strengthen. To declare to be true.

agnosticism The theory that, while not denying the existence of God, asserts that God cannot be known and that only objective phenomena are objects of real knowledge.

ashram A secluded, quiet place for study and spiritual practice that provides a supportive environment where spiritual aspirants can live without distractions.

astral realm The realm of life forces and energies.

astrology The study of the positions and aspects of planets and their possible influence on the course of human affairs.

atheism Disbelief in or denial of the existence of God.

avatar A complete incarnation of divine qualities and powers. A spiritually enlightened soul that incarnates to impart divine influences into human affairs and planetary consciousness. The impersonal "universal avatar" concept is that divine qualities of individuals are unveiled and become increasingly influential as individual and collective consciousness becomes illumined.

awareness Our awareness reflects perceptions to our mind and consciousness. When our awareness is blurred and perceptions are not accurate, illusions can result. Skillful use of powers of discriminative intelligence enables us to avoid illusions.

ayurveda Sanskrit *ayus*, life; *veda*, knowledge. A natural way to nurture total well-being that evolved in India thousands of years ago. Diagnostic procedures include examination of the patient's pulse, body temperature, skin, eyes, psychological characteristics, mental attitude, behaviors, and other factors. Treatment may include foods and herbs for specific purposes, attitude adjustment, behavior modification, detoxification regimens, meditation practice, and other procedures used to restore balance to the basic mind-body constitution.

The basic mind-body constitution is regulated by three subtle governing principles (vata, space-air; pitta, fire; kapha, water-earth). Foods are chosen according to their tastes (sweet, sour, salty, pungent, bitter, astringent). Food transformation is said to progress through eight stages: plasma, blood, muscle, fat, bone, bone marrow, reproductive essences, and a refined energy that strengthens the immune system.

In the *Charaka Samhita*, a primary ayurvedic text, medicinal uses of more than five hundred herbs are described. Knowledge of ayurvedic practices spread from India to Tibet, China, and Mediterranean countries, and more recently to Europe and the Americas. During the years of British rule in India, ayurvedic practices declined in urban areas but continued to be the health treatment of choice among rural populations. Several ayurvedic colleges in India have been established in recent years and clinics in many countries provide ayurvedic services.

Siddha medicine, a similar wellness system, evolved in south India. Its many treatises are believed to have been written by enlightened saints (*siddhas*), among whom Agastya is especially revered. Practitioners of this system also prescribe the ashes of gems and purified metals for healing and rejuvenation.

Bhagavad Gita Holy or divine song (*bhaj*, to revere or love, *gai*, song). It is a story in which each character, object, and event symbolically illustrates an ideal or moral or religious principle. Krishna, one of the central characters, represents enlightened consciousness that reveals to the truth seeker (Arjuna) "the eternal way of righteousness" with emphasis on knowledge, selfless service, devotion, and meditation.

bliss The pure joy of awareness of being rather than a happy mental state or an emotional feeling or mood.

buddhi Verb-root *budh*, to know. A spiritually enlightened person is said to be a buddha, one who knows the truth about life. Because souls are units of one Reality, everyone has a "buddha nature" at the core of their being.

capacity The ability to receive, hold, or absorb.

categories of cosmic manifestation Yoga practices are based on a philosophical system that numbers the categories and defines the processes of cosmic manifestation. Supreme Consciousness eternally exists. Its absolute aspect is changeless; its expressive aspect is subject to change in accord with the states of its primary attributes (*gunas*) which regulate cosmic forces. When the three gunas are in a state of equilibrium, manifestation of cosmic forces does not occur. When tamas guna (inertia) is influential, a vibration of the power of supreme Consciousness is emanated in which time, space, and fine cosmic forces are produced. From the unified field of primordial Nature, electric and magnetic forces are projected as five subtle element-influences: space with cosmic forces that have the potential to form as matter; air (gaseous elements); fire; water; and earth, which interact to produce physical matter. The five fine element-influences are called the true essences of the material universe. Manifestation of the elements is said to occur when half of a subtle element-influence combines with one eighth of a part of each of the other four element-influences.

causal realm The cosmic, electric, and magnetic forces emanated from the field of primordial Nature that produce the astral and physical realms.

chakras Sanskrit "wheels." The seven major astral centers in the spine and brain, each with unique attributes.

The first chakra at the base of the spine has the earth-element attribute. The prana-frequency taste is sweet. The color is yellow. The sound is as restless buzzing of bees. Sanskrit *muladhara*, "foundation." A psychological characteristic of this chakra is stability.

Second chakra, at the sacrum of the spine. Water-element. The taste is astringent. The color is white. The sound is like that of a flute. Sanskrit *swadhisthana*, "abode of ordinary self-consciousness." A characteristic influence is sensualness.

Third chakra, at the lumbar region of the spine opposite the navel. Fire-element. The taste is bitter. The color is red. The sound is like that of a harp. Sanskrit *manipura*, "the city of jewels." When awareness is identified here, one may express self-control and fervent aspiration to spiritual growth.

Categories of Cosmic Manifestation

Field of Absolute (Pure) Consciousness

Supreme Consciousness with Attributes (God)

Field of Primordial Nature
Om, space, time, and fine cosmic forces.
Interactions between supreme Consciousness and the field of
primordial Nature produce individualized units of pure
consciousness (souls).

Cosmic Mind
Of which all individual minds are units and which is
responsive to our mental states, thoughts, and desires.

Causal Realm (Electromagnetic Forces)

Astral Realm (Electromagnetic Forces and Life Forces)

Physical Realm
Produced by interactions of subtle element influences:
space with cosmic forces; air (gaseous substances);
fire (transformative influence); water (lubricating,
nourishing characteristics); earth (dense matter
of confined energy). The physical and psychological
characteristics of living things are governed by the
influences of three constituent attributes that
pervade the universe.

Note: See *categories of cosmic manifestation*, *gunas*,
and *mind-body constitution*.

Fourth chakra, at the dorsal region of the spine between the shoulder blades. Air element. The taste is sour. The color is blue. The sound is like a continuous peal of a gong. Sanskrit *anahata*, "unstruck sound." When identified here, one has mastery of the senses and life forces.

Fifth chakra, at the cervical region of the spine, opposite the throat. Ether (space) element. The taste is pungent. The color is gray or misty with sparkling points of white light. The sound is like an ocean's roar. Sanskrit *vishudda*, "pure." When awareness is identified here, one may have exceptional powers of intellectual and intuitive discernment.

Sixth chakra, between the eyebrows, the spiritual eye center associated with the front lobes of the brain. Life forces flowing upward and focused here may be perceived as a dark blue orb with a golden halo and a silver-white light in the field of blue. Gold is considered to be the energy-frequency of Om; dark blue, the frequency of all-pervading Consciousness within creation; the white, starlike light is that of Consciousness beyond relative phenomena. Sanskrit *ajna*: decisive power of will or intention, command or control.

Seventh chakra: Related, but not confined to the higher brain. Pure consciousness and transcendence of mental and physical states and of all conditions that modify or distort awareness. Sanskrit *sahasrara*, "thousand rayed."

channeling A modern word for mediumship: the belief that souls which have departed from this world can be contacted by telepathic or other means for the purpose of communication. Some people try to contact souls in astral realms to prove their existence in the hope of obtaining higher knowledge. People who claim to be able to do this are either self-deceived or dishonest. They should concentrate on actualizing their own divine qualities.

chant A simple, melodic lyric repeatedly intoned or sung. Studies have revealed that chanting can reduce stress, calm the mind, and result in harmonious interactions between the hemispheres of the brain.

compassion Empathetic concern for the suffering or misfortune of others together with an inclination to give aid or support.

concentration An undisturbed flow of attention.

conscience The ability to recognize the difference between right and wrong regarding one's conduct, with knowledge that one should act accordingly. Compliant conformance to one's sense of proper conduct.

consciousness In ordinary usage: awareness of self-identity and the totality of feelings, attitudes, opinions, beliefs, what is known to be true, and the quality and degree of our tendencies and capacities to be influenced by external conditions and be either reactive or responsive to them. Metaphysical usage: the essence of what we are, our real, inherent, unchanging nature. Supreme Consciousness is the essence of the one, supreme Reality.

contemplate From Latin *com*, intensive; *templum*, a space for observing something. To examine, ponder, or consider as being possible. To hopefully look at with expectation of discovery.

cosmic consciousness Awareness and understanding of the unified wholeness of life.

cosmic mind The one, universal mind of which all minds are units or parts. Our mental states, subliminal tendencies and urges, thoughts, desires, and intentions interact with cosmic mind which is inclined to responsively express or manifest corresponding circumstances.

decisive Characterized by determined or resolute choice.

deism The belief that God created the universe, but is apart from it, has no influence on phenomena, and provides no revelation.

delusion An erroneous idea, concept, or belief.

desire To wish for or want. Desires enable us to achieve goals and accomplish purposes. Life-enhancing desires that contribute to our well-being are acceptable. Nonuseful desires or obsessive cravings that interfere with rational thinking, cause emotional unrest, or are allowed to impel unwise or erratic behaviors should be avoided or replaced with wholesome, life-enhancing desires.

devotion Strong attraction. Attachment or loyalty.

dharma That which upholds and supports the processes of life and empowers evolution. Dharmic living is life lived in harmony with the cosmic order. To adhere to one's path in life in accord with the orderly processes of Nature is to fulfill one's dharma: purposes that are constructive and meaningful.

disciple Latin *discipulus*; from *discere*, to learn. An adherent of a philosophical system or spiritual tradition.

ego An illusional (mistaken) sense of Self that causes and sustains a false sense of identity. When the ego is purified, we are aware of being a unit of pure consciousness and the ego as a viewpoint from which to dispassionately observe objective and subjective phenomena.

egotism An inflated sense of self-importance which may result in a strong sense of individualism and arrogant willfulness.

elicit To bring forth. Relaxation, mental calmness, spiritual qualities, and superconscious states are elicited by meditation practice.

emotion A subjective feeling-response to something observed or experienced. Thoughts, memories, smells, tastes, the behaviors or words of others, and objective events or circumstances that are observed or experienced may elicit feelings of aversion, fear, insecurity, sadness, loneliness, desire, confidence, happiness, security, well-being, compassion, attraction, or other emotional responses that are mild, medium, or strong. Emotional stability and maturity provides a firm foundation for spiritual growth.

enlightenment To provide with spiritual wisdom or insight.

era A duration of time. See *yuga*.

evolution A process, usually gradual, in which something changes into a different and usually better or more complex form. Spiritual evolution can be quickened by right, concentrated endeavor.

faith Confident belief in the truth, value, or trustworthiness of something. Belief not based on proof or material evidence. Religious or spiritual conviction.

field Metaphysical usage: something in which events can occur. Our awareness is a field. Cosmic mind is a field. The Oversoul aspect of supreme Consciousness and the realm of primordial Nature are fields. Physics: a region of space indicated by physical properties such as gravitational or electromagnetic forces.

God The absolute aspect is pure existence-being devoid of any distinguishing characteristics. The expressive aspect (Godhead or Oversoul) has constituent attributes (*gunas*) which pervade its emanated, vibrating power (Om) and the universe.

The word *god* (German "the highest good") is derived from an Indo-European language in which an ancestor form meant "the invoked one." The only surviving non-Germanic relative is Sanskrit *hu* ("invoke the Gods"), a form which is in the Rig-Veda (Hymn of Knowledge) as *puruhutas* ("much invoked"). The Sanskrit word Brahma is used to refer to the expanding, creation-producing aspect of supreme Consciousness. Brahman is used to indicate absolute supreme Consciousness.

Muslims who are devoted to the ideal of submission to God use the word Allah (al-Lah), The Great Adored. Many Christians use the words God, Heavenly Father, and Lord.

The names used to refer to God reflect what people imagine to be the highest attribute of deity. Zoroastrians in ancient Persia (Iran) used Ahura Mazda, The Wise Creator. In Hinduism, some aspects of deity are characterized according to their presumed influences or roles: Divine Mother, a nurturing influence; Ishwara, that which rules or regulates the cosmic order; Shiva, transformative, regenerative influence; Vishnu, that which preserves; Saraswati, goddess of speech and learning; Lakshmi, goddess of prosperity and good fortune. Goddesses are depicted as the creative energies of the gods (the cosmic forces and their unique influences).

Godhead The Oversoul aspect of supreme Consciousness which emanates the vibrating power (Om) that produces and sustains universes.

grace Freely given benefits, good fortune, provision or support.

gunas The three constituent attributes of the aspect of supreme Consciousness that pervades the primordial field of Nature and a universe and regulates cosmic forces. Their influences are: 1) *sattwic*, elevating and illuminating; 2) *rajasic*, transformative; 3) *tamasic*, inertial.

guru That which removes (*ru*) darkness or ignorance (*gu*). A teacher. In enlightenment traditions a guru is viewed as a conduit through which higher knowledge and transformative spiritual force can be transmitted to the receptive disciple.

hallucination A false or distorted perception of objects or events. Mind- or brain-produced phenomena without any real basis.

heal To make whole. To restore to complete health, wellness, or spiritual wholeness.

heart The physical heart is the hollow, muscular organ in the thoracic cavity that pumps blood. Metaphysical: the essence of one's being and sensibilities, the true Self. When seers advise us to "seek the truth in our heart" they mean that the core essence of our being is to be meditatively contemplated, discovered, and experienced.

heaven Originally a cosmological term used to refer to a region of the universe, which was later used to denote religious idealism. In ancient Middle Eastern thought, heaven was imagined as a region of the observable cosmos beyond which was a transcendent realm. In ancient Greek mythology, Zeus was depicted as dwelling on Mount Olympus. Writers of the books of The Old Testament referred to heaven as God's abode from which sovereign rule was exercised and to which the faithful righteous would be eventually welcomed. The New Testament indicates a modified version of heaven as a creation of God in which God resides, as well as a final condition of blessedness to be experienced by the spiritually prepared. Christian sects have varied concepts of heaven.

Hinduism A word coined by foreigners who invaded India. The river Sindu, flowing into the Arabian Sea and forming a part of the western boundary of India, was referred to by the ancient Persians as the *Hindu* River. The Greeks borrowed the name, changing it to "Indos," which was later converted into English "Indus." The Greeks referred to the country east of the "Indos" as India. Its people became known as Hindus and their cultural and religious practices as Hinduism. The traditional name of their practices is *Sanatana Dharma*, "The Eternal Way of Right Living," because they are in accord with the laws of cosmic order. India is known to its people as Bharatavarsha or Bharat, derived from the name of an ancient king.

holistic Emphasis on the importance of the wholeness of something and the interdependence of its parts and processes.

holy Of divine origin or character.

humility Absence of egotism.

illusion Latin *illusio*, an imitation or counterfeit of something. A mistaken perception of subjective or objective reality: of thoughts, concepts, feelings, or external things or events.

imagination A mental picture or concept of something which does not yet exist. Fantasy is unregulated imagination.

initiation Latin *initium*, beginning; from *inire*, to go in. A new beginning. A rite of passage into a body of knowledge and the company of adherents of that knowledge.

inspire Latin *inspirare*: in-, *into*, and *spirare*, to breath. To be inspired is to be affected, or aroused by divine influence.

intellect The faculty of discrimination or discernment.

intensive Concentrated, focused.

intuition Direct perception without the aid of the senses.

karma Any influence that may cause an effect. Accumulated subconscious conditionings and tendencies, mental attitudes, behaviors, inclinations, expectations, and desires are aspects of one's personal karmic condition. Karmic conditions that are troublesome can be resisted, weakened, and neutralized by constructive thinking, feeling, and behaviors, and regular practice of superconscious meditation.

kriya A Sanskrit word for an action or process that can produce a desired effect.

kriya yoga Disciplined thinking and behavior, discovery of one's essence of being, and devotional surrender to God (seeing through or transcending illusional ideas of Self). Intensive (concentrated) practice enables rapid spiritual growth to be experienced.

kundalini Soul force, which is mostly dormant in people who are not yet spiritually awake. In spiritually awake individuals, its energies are enlivening and transformative. They are aroused by aspiration to spiritual growth, devotion, meditation, being in places where spiritual influences are strong, and mental and spiritual attunement with an enlightened person.

life The property or quality manifested in growth, metabolism, response to stimuli, and reproduction. The physical, mental, and spiritual experiences that make up our sense of existence.

light Electromagnetic radiation. It travels at 186,282 miles a second. The sun's radiation travels 93 million miles to our planet in approximately eight minutes, where we perceive it as light when it impacts the planet's atmosphere. The wavelengths that produce red, orange, yellow, green, blue, indigo and violet colors are visible to humans. Red is generally believed to be produced by a low frequency, long wave; violet by a high frequency, short wave. TV, FM, and radio frequencies are below red; ultraviolet, X-rays and gamma rays are beyond violet. All electromagnetic frequencies, visible and invisible, are light. When an electron in an atom is impacted by radiation or collides with another atom, it receives energy which it either absorbs or emits as a photon (particle) of light of a specific wavelength.

love Intense affection (fondness) for someone or a living thing.

mantra Sanskrit *manas*, mind, and *tra*, to protect. A word, word-phrase, or sound used to focus attention, especially when meditating.

master Latin *magister*. One who is acknowledged as being proficient in a branch of learning or has unique skills or abilities. A master of yoga (samadhi) has control over his or her sensory impulses, vital forces, mental and emotional states, and states of consciousness.

material A substance of which something is made.

matter Confined energy that occupies space.

maya That which measures, defines, limits, and produces forms of matter; characteristics of the primordial field of Nature.

meditation An undisturbed flow of attention to an object or ideal one aspires to identify with or realize. Detachment of attention and awareness from external conditions, the senses, emotions, and mental states that enables one to realize their pure-conscious essence of being and the reality of God.

metaphysics Latin *metaphysica* < Greek *tà metà tà physiká*, "the things after the physics," the title given to Aristotle's treatise on first principles that followed his treatise on physics. The branch of philosophy that investigates the first principles of ultimate reality, including the nature of being and cosmology.

mind Sanskrit *manas*, to think. Our mind processes perceptions and organizes information.

mind-body constitution Formed by inherited characteristics, prenatal and postnatal environmental influences, and one's karmic condition when born. The three governing principles (*doshas*) of biological and psychological processes are vata (air or flowing movements); pitta (fire, that influences chemical, biological, and psychological transformation); kapha (moisture and dense substances that provide support, lubrication, and nourishment). Indications of balanced vata influences are efficient elimination of waste products, sound sleep, a strong immune system, orderly functioning of the body's systems, and emotional stability. Indications of balanced pita influences are strong powers of digestion, vitality, decisiveness, keen powers of intelligence, self-confidence, and courage. Indications of balanced kapha influences are physical strength, serenity, firm mental resolve, rational thinking, patience, endurance, and adaptability to circumstances. When the mind-body constitution is balanced, physical and psychological health prevails. When it is not balanced, physical or psychological distress may be experienced. Balance can be restored by attitude adjustment, behavior modification, diet, appropriate therapeutic regimens, and cultivation of spiritual awareness. See *ayurveda*.

miracle An event that seems impossible to explain by natural laws because the natural laws that caused it are not generally known.

modify To change the character of something, limit, or restrict. Our ordinary awareness is modified by acquired information, erroneous ideas (delusions), misperceptions (illusions), sleep, memories, and fantasies. Superconsciousness is unmodified.

mysticism Spiritual discipline practiced to unify attention and awareness with one's true nature and God or ultimate reality, usually by means of contemplative meditation. The experience of such realization. Belief in the existence of realities beyond ordinary powers of perception which are accessible by subjective experience, as by intuition.

nadi A channel or pathway through which prana (life force) flows. Ida nadi is the left channel along the spine, the lunar influence. Pingala is the right channel, the solar influence. Sushumna nadi, the central channel, is the path through which vital forces ascend when attention is internalized or when certain meditation methods (such as kriya pranayama) are used. Within sushumna nadi are two astral channels and a fine channel of consciousness-matter.

ojas A fine energy that strengthens the body's immune system. The final product of food transformation. It is increased by mental calmness, wholesome living, spiritual practices, and conservation and transmutation of vital forces.

Om (AUM) The vibration of the power of Consciousness.

omnipotence Unlimited power.

omnipresence Present everywhere.

omniscience All knowing.

Oversoul See *Godhead*.

paramahansa *Para*, beyond, transcendent; *hansa*, swan. One who is considered to be a spiritual master, a free soul no longer limited by karma or illusions and whose wisdom-impelled actions are always appropriate. As a swan has an earthly abode and can soar free in the sky, so a paramahansa dwells in the world but is not confined by it. According to mythology, a swan is able to extract milk from a mixture of milk and water. A paramahansa partakes of the divine essence while living without restrictions in the world.

patience   Calm endurance of circumstances by being peacefully soul-centered.

philosophy   Latin *philosophia* < Greek *philosophos*. The love and seeking of wisdom by diligent inquiry and self-discipline.

prana   Life force. The soul's life force flows into the body at the medulla oblongata at the base of the brain. When prana flows freely, health prevails. When flows of prana are imbalanced, weak, or disturbed, psychological and physical discomfort or distress may occur. Pranayama practice harmonizes flows of prana in the body.

pranayama   *Prana,* life force that is *ayama*, not restrained. The practice of pranayama usually involves regulation of breathing rhythms to harmonize flows of life force in the body and calm the mind as preparation for meditation practice.

prayer   Latin *precaria*, to obtain by entreaty or earnest request. The act of making such a request. Usually reverent petitioning of God for something that is desired or needed. Motivation for prayer ranges from desire for material benefit to the hope of union with God. One's prayer style may be vocal, mental, or wordless aspiration. Forms of prayer may be of acknowledgment, thanksgiving, confession, asking for help of some kind, or intercession. Contemplative prayer is simple, surrendered awareness of the presence of God, without words or concepts. When a sense of God-communion is not felt, one can patiently, silently sit with knowledge that God is real. The more conscious we are of abiding in God, the less inclined we are to ask God for anything. When our awareness of our relationship with God is constant, supportive events and circumstances that are for our highest good and the highest good of others often spontaneously and effortlessly unfold.

primordial Nature   The first field of cosmic manifestation in which Om and its self-manifested aspects—space, time, and fine cosmic forces—are unified.

prosperity   Continuous unfoldments of fortunate events and ideal circumstances that spontaneously occur when the spiritual, mental, emotional, physical, and environmental components of our lives are harmoniously integrated.

psyche In most Western cultures the *psyche* (Latin from Greek *psykhe*, soul) is usually viewed as the mind being the center of thought, feeling, and behavior, and adjusting and relating the body to its social and physical environment.

psychic Of or relating to the soul or to extraordinary powers of perception or ability.

realization Comprehension, to experience and know.

redemptive The capacity to restore, rescue, free, or liberate.

reincarnation Physical rebirth of souls because of necessity or inclinations to have experiences in the physical realm. It is not spiritually beneficial to be preoccupied with past incarnations. Attention and endeavors should instead be focused on authentic spiritual growth that will result in liberation of consciousness.

renunciation Letting go of mental and emotional attachments to things, circumstances, emotional states, memories, actions, and the results of actions. This is most easily done by concentrating on purposes that have real value.

sage A wise person.

saint A person whose divine qualities are expressive.

salvation Freedom from pain, discomfort, or ignorance which may be temporary or permanent in accord with one's degree of spiritual awareness. Limited salvation is a confined condition: Self-realization may not be complete. Subliminal inclinations or erroneous beliefs or illusions may still be influential. When all limitations are absent, salvation is absolute and permanent.

samadhi The "bringing together completely" of attention and awareness with an object or ideal of meditative contemplation. During preliminary samadhi, attention and awareness are supported by an object of perception. Higher (pure) samadhi is not supported by an object.

Sanskrit The refined ("polished") language from which more than one hundred Indo-European languages have been derived. Prominent in

India during the Vedic era, it is again being more widely studied and used. The Sanskrit alphabet is considered to be a mantra with sound-phrases of spiritual significance and power which contain the seed-frequencies of creation. Every sound (*shabda*) has a power (*shakti*) which conveys a meaning which is inseparably related to the sound. The sound-element behind the audible sounds is the fundamental sound (*sphota*). Contemplation of a subtle sound-element or seed (*bija*) reveals its true essence. Sanskrit mantras are believed to be unique when used to facilitate spiritual awakening. Their potency is derived from Om, the primordial sound current emanating from the Godhead and expressive in and as the universe.

satan Many religious people have attempted to define an array of unseen presences which are imagined as having power to affect human beings and circumstances: gods, demigods, angels, devils, demons, fairies, and ghosts. Some of these imaginary influences are viewed as benevolent; others are viewed as harmful. The ancient Hebrew word, satan, meant "obstructor" or something which causes difficulties. When the Old Testament was translated into Greek in the third century B.C.E., *satan* was translated as *diabolus* (French *diable*; German *Teuful*; English *devil*). The first known endeavor to concentrate all evil in a single, personal form occurred before the sixth century B.C.E., in Persia: given the name Ahiriman and described as the Principle of Darkness engaged in ceaseless conflict for control of the world with the Principle of Light. This concept of a personified evil influence was adapted from Persian ideas by Jewish religious thinkers and later by early Christians. The fact that satanic influences do not exist has not yet persuaded millions of people to abandon this erroneous idea.

science Disciplined observation, precise identification, and experimental investigation of mundane phenomena or other realities.

seer One who accurately discerns the truth of what is observed.

Self An individualized unit of pure consciousness; our essence of being. Our true nature, rather than the illusional sense of selfhood (egocentric self-consciousness). When identified with matter, a Self is referred to as a soul. Units of pure consciousness are individualized by interactions between supreme Consciousness and primordial Nature.

Self-realization is actualized when the difference between one's pure essence of being and ordinary awareness is experienced.

shakti The expressive energy of kundalini.

shaktipat Arousal of kundalini energies which may spontaneously occur or can occur because of mental and spiritual attunement or physical contact with someone whose energies are already active.

siddha A spiritually accomplished person. *Siddhis* are exceptional powers of perception or extraordinary abilities that may be elicited as one becomes more spiritually conscious.

soul A unit of pure consciousness with blurred awareness that is not aware of its pure-conscious essence. Souls that become involved with matter have four characteristics: ego-consciousness (a false sense of self); the ability to be aware of objects of perception; a mind; and intelligence, the capacity to discriminate.

space The infinite extension of three-dimensional reality in which events occur.

spiritual Of or related to God and souls.

spiritual eye The sixth chakra, located in the forehead between and above the eyebrows. Light may be perceived here when a meditator's mind is calm. See *chakra*.

stage A level, degree, or period of time in the course of a process.

subjective Produced by or existing in the mind.

subliminal Below conscious awareness. Subliminal drives and tendencies activate thoughts and emotions. When they cease to be influential, the mind is calm and awareness is clear.

superconscious Latin *super*, above. A clear state of consciousness.

swami A member of the ancient monastic order reorganized by the philosopher-seer Adi (the first) Shankara in the seventh century. A swami renounces all mundane attachments, selflessly works for the highest good of others, and (usually) engages in spiritual practices.

technique A systematic procedure. A meditation technique can be used to elicit relaxation, calm the mind, and focus attention.

time An interval between events. A part of a continuum which includes space and cosmic forces, no part of which can be distinguished from the others except by arbitrary division for the purpose of analysis or theoretical speculation.

Our concept of time is related to things and events: pendulums swing; quartz crystals vibrate; atoms, light waves, electric and magnetic fields, and planets move. But what is time like where nothing exists? In an absolute void only the Something that makes relative happenings possible exists.

The interval of time we call a year marks one movement of the earth around the sun; a day is one spin of the earth on its axis; a month was once related to the duration of the orbit of the moon. Astronomical measures of time are not absolute. The moon is farther away from the earth than it was many thousands of years ago. Days and years are variable happenings rather than exact markings of time. A seven-day week is an arbitrary designation. Different cultures have had five, eight, and ten day weeks.

Until the fourteenth century, days were divided into irregular intervals of morning, noon, evening, and night. Summer daylight hours are longer than winter daylight hours. Hours, minutes, and time zones began to be standardized only a few centuries ago when it became necessary to coordinate train schedules.

At the Equator, the earth's rate of spin is 1,000 miles an hour. Its speed around the sun is almost 20 miles a second (72,000 miles an hour). Our solar system in relationship to the center of our galaxy is moving at the rate of 120 miles a second (432,000 miles an hour). Our galaxy is moving toward another galaxy (Andromeda) at 50 miles a second (180,000 miles an hour).

Time need not be thought of as an insurmountable obstacle to spiritual growth. Refinements of the nervous system, and other physical changes that may be necessary to accommodate higher states of consciousness, occur in time.

transcendental Rising above common thoughts, ideas, or states of consciousness.

Transcendental Field Absolute (pure) Consciousness. Referred to as existence-being because it does not have attributes. That which is to be ultimately realized.

transcendentalism The belief that understanding or knowledge of higher realities is intuitively perceived rather than acquired only by examination of objective circumstances.

veda Knowledge.

Vedas The oldest known religious scriptures which emerged in India more than five thousand years ago. The common theme in Vedic literature is that one Reality exists and can be known.

wisdom The understanding of what is true, right, or enduring.

yantra A symbolic geometrical drawing used as a focus for meditative contemplation that depicts the actions and influences of cosmic forces. Favored by many yogis is Sri Yantra, composed of circles, triangles, lotus petals, and mantras within a square that contains the energies. The design symbolically portrays the interactions of Shiva and Shakti: supreme Consciousness and its creative powers.

yoga Sanskrit *yug*, to yoke, to join. Samadhi, the meaning used in Patanjali's yoga-sutras. Practice that enables a person to be Self- and God-realized.

yuga An era or designated duration of time. Many centuries ago, Vedic astronomer-seers taught a theory of time-cycles to explain the effects of cosmic forces on human beings and the emergence and decline of civilizations. An ascending cycle is half of a complete 24,000 year cycle:

• 1,200 years of a Dark Age of confusion during which most people are intellectually deficient and spiritually unaware. The last Dark Age ended circa 1700 in our current era.
• 2,400 years during which the intellectual powers and spiritual capacities of people increase and the electric and magnetic properties of Nature are discovered and used. We are a little over 300 years into a 2,400-year ascending cycle, which will continue until 4100 C.E.
• 3,600 years during which the mental and intellectual powers of at

least fifty percent of the global human population are highly developed. This era will continue until 7700 C.E.

• 4,800 years during which at least seventy-five percent of the people on our planet are spiritually conscious and many of them are spiritually enlightened. This era will continue until 12,500 C.E.

This theory of cosmic time-cycles, first published by Sri Yukteswar in 1895, is based on the idea that forces from the center of our galaxy influence the electromagnetic fields of the solar system and the mental and intellectual faculties of its human inhabitants. When our solar system is most distant from the center of our galaxy, the mental, intellectual, and intuitive powers of many people are weak, soul awareness is dim, and inability to comprehend the facts of life is common. When our solar system is nearest to the galactic center, mental, intellectual, and intuitive powers of more people become highly developed and their spiritual capacities are unveiled.

Because a mistake was made (circa 700 B.C.E.) in calculating the progression of time-cycles, many people still erroneously believe that we are in a Dark Age of confusion.

The consciousness and behaviors of dedicated spiritual aspirants need not be unduly influenced by external events; their mental, intellectual, and intuitive powers can be developed regardless of the era in which they live.

For free information about meditation retreats,
seminars, and books by Roy Eugene Davis, contact:

Center for Spiritual Awareness
Post Office Box 7
Lakemont, Georgia 30552-0001

Telephone 706-782-4723
Fax 706-782-4560

e-mail: csainc@csa-davis.org
Internet web site: www.csa-davis.org